# COLLEC...
# PICTURE PO...
# —an introduction

by
## Anthony Byatt, F.S.C.A.

Golden Age Postcard Books
Malvern, Worcs.

First Published in 1982 by Golden Age Postcard Books
28 St, Peter's Road, Malvern, Worcs. WR14 1QS.

British Library Cataloguing in Publication Data
    Byatt, Anthony,
    Collecting Picture Postcards—An Introduction
    1. Postal Cards—Collectors and collecting
    769.5      NC 1872
    ISBN 0 9506212 1 8.
*By the same author:*
    Picture Postcards and Their Publishers, 1978.

Made and printed in Great Britain by
Adams & Sons (Printers) Ltd., Hereford.

# Contents

# 1   Why Collect Picture Postcards?

Today it is easy to say everything with pictures; the television screen, the cinema, and numerous picture books and magazines all speak to us with the picture. But seventy to eighty years ago the situation was very different, and the humble postcard was one of the best means of sending a message with a picture. Most cards cost one penny or less, and then could be posted with a halfpenny stamp in England, for one cent in the United States or five cents in France. When its collecting possibilities were realised as well, postcard publishers everywhere quickly responded by producing such a wide variety of postcards, that it would be foolish for anyone to say that a particular subject has never appeared on a picture postcard. When this has happened—and kites, Guy Fawkes' Night and Morris Dancers have been three of these subjects—collectors have soon found a number of cards to disprove it.

Here is the first reason for collecting picture postcards today. Whatever your interests, you can assemble a number of cards around any theme you wish and almost every angle of that theme can be depicted. Some subjects can be dealt with adequately with a few dozen cards, but, for a wider theme, you could soon have a thousand cards and a few collectors have amassed more than a million—they could quite well be called 'Postcard Millionaires'. If you already have a hobby which continues to claim your attention, then why not add postcards to it, for they will help to illustrate its many features. So, if you collect stamps or coins or pressed flowers, you can find a wealth of picture postcards to set off these collections. If you like music, the theatre or the cinema, you can collect pictures of composers, musicians, stage and film personalities and their many productions. For those with a love of past times or a desire to see the world, there are endless possibilities.

It is perhaps the nostalgic appeal that is strongest when it comes to collecting picture postcards. Whilst we are very well aware of our present situation, we have an insatiable curiosity to not only peep into the future but also to try and find a time-machine into which we can climb to trace back through the years, and particularly those years we can still hear little tit-bits about from our grandparents. Here is that time-machine within our grasp, ready to be tailored to suit our exact requirements.

Another reason is not so obvious to those who are familiar with modern picture postcards which seem to display a certain uniformity of style and printing. Not so the picture postcards of yesteryear, for they come in a vast range that quite bewilders the person who is used to only holiday views and rude seaside comics. The beautiful printing and colouring techniques used during the postcard's Golden Age (1900–1918) would be prohibitive in cost today. Many cards were hand-coloured by teams of girls who were paid a few pence for a thousand cards. The chromo-lithograph made on stone

5

represents the height of achievement in early colour printing. Postcards printed by this method are amongst the most expensive for collectors today, yet they are truly works of art in their own right, and when a superb design was used the combination is most attractive and adds yet another reason for starting a picture postcard collection.

Finally, in these difficult times of inflation when it costs too much to sweep the streets, never mind paving them with gold, the investment potential of postcards cannot be forgotten. The genuine postcard collector or cartologist (in America deltiologist, in France cartophilist) never considers this aspect first and foremost, and collects the cards he wants to and likes. But as his knowledge increases, he learns to buy cards at the best price, even where they do not particularly appeal to him. If he can acquire a good card at a cheap price, he knows that he can trade or exchange it for others he would like to keep.

With the older hobbies, such as stamp collecting, there is a vast reservoir of knowledge available which, through the years, has explored almost every nook and cranny. But postcard collecting almost died out in the 1920s, and during the thirty years that followed, many publishers' records were lost or destroyed, especially during World War II. So it is very much a matter of picking up the pieces today and slowly trying to re-assemble them. In itself this is another reason for collecting picture postcards for those who like the excitement of putting together a story long forgotten, or rediscovering the work of an artist long since dead. This last potential is truly great, for the work of thousands of artists is recorded on picture postcards, and though few of us would have either the money or room to house a collection of paintings, we can assemble their work in miniature whether it is recorded on just a few hundred postcards, or on several thousands for the more prolific artists.

So there are any number of reasons why collecting picture postcards makes sense. They are most versatile, covering every subject we can think of. They can serve as an addition to other hobbies. They remind us of past interesting and perhaps happier times. They are beautiful works of art in themselves, and they can provide an investment in addition. In the following pages, we will explore together this vast array of subjects so that you can make the best choice of what you personally would like to collect.

# 2    Familiar Streets and Landmarks

When collectors are asked which sort of card is most popular, there is no complete agreement, but the so-called 'topographical' type is always very high on the list. It is a pity this term is so widely used for I find it cumbersome. They are the cards that depict our own locality, the town or village which is so familiar to us, its streets, prominent buildings and landmarks.

Some people have never moved from the place where they were born or at least they still live in the same county, state or province. If this is so you may only want to collect cards of this particular area. But, if at some time, you have moved to an entirely different part of the country, you may have grown to love that place just as much as the town in which you were born. So now you may want to have two entirely separate collections, both running along the same lines but otherwise not connected. This is where you can please yourself and can limit or extend your collection according to your interests and your pocket.

What should you look for in building up a topographical collection? An important feature will obviously be the street scenes and the more detail shown in them the better. Those with plenty of people and traffic moving about are the most popular, especially where the scene has radically changed with the passing of the years. Other things to look for include shops and their contents, shop signs and owners' names, street signs and furniture, and changes in the buildings. Through a magnifying glass it is surprising what can be picked out if the reproduction is clear.

Let us consider an interesting example of alterations to buildings which has entirely changed a well-known street scene. We go to the town of Stratford-on-Avon, home of Shakespeare, known to millions of tourists from all parts of the world. This is in Chapel Street, just a few yards from the site of the house to which Shakespeare retired in 1610, with the adjacent museum and the charming knot garden. Our picture *(illustration 1)* shows the Shakespeare Hotel as it is today, and we would have to be an expert in architecture to distinguish the original contemporary timber-framed buildings from the mock Tudor frontages.

But now examine the second *illustration* and all is revealed. Called 'Ye Five Gables' seventy years ago, we are able to pick out recent careful restoration of the windows on the first and second floors and more particularly the ground floor. Notice the early postcard shop 'W. Stanton, Artistic printer, Bookseller and Stationer', which has long since disappeared. Now look beyond the five original gables and see the entire rebuilding that has taken place around the original main entrance to the Hotel. Four more gables have been added and the rest of the frontage has been built to match, even the sign that swings from the timber arm. Finally, the ancient gas lamp has been replaced by a taller electric street light.

7

*The Shakespeare Hotel as seen today (courtesy J. Salmon Ltd.).*

*The same scene more than sixty years ago.*

*Morley's Hotel in Trafalgar Square, London, some sixty years ago.*

*A Norfolk street scene full of life and interest.*

Another example can be found in London's well-known Trafalgar Square, where on the East side, near the famous Church of Saint Martin's-in-the-Fields, stands South Africa House. Our third *illustration* shows the same spot when it was occupied by Morley's Hotel, which was acquired in 1921 and subsequently demolished. The tree in the foreground of the picture looking young and of slender girth is now quite a considerable size. This picture was taken by Lewis of Nottingham, a publisher noted for his detailed views of Central London. For places like this it is easy to find a modern postcard for purposes of comparison, but if you should have difficulty in doing this, why not take your own postcard-size photograph by standing in the same place as the photographer of seventy or eighty years ago!

Prices vary considerably for street scenes, according to the amount of activity shown in the picture and also depending on how much that street was photographed. The main streets of large cities will be the cheapest followed by the main streets of provincial towns and then of villages. Some suburban streets can be the most costly for many of them were rarely photographed, and then usually to a special order by a particular person whose house takes pride of place in the foreground, and who perhaps bought three or four dozen postcard prints from the local photographer. So do not despise the completely anonymous postcard view, for sometimes it can be one of the scarcest. It is just unfortunate that many of these cards don't give the name of the street or town either and if you are fortunate enough to recognise one of them in a dealer's 'mystery' section you may be able to buy it quite cheaply.

Very similar to this last kind of street scene are the many pictures of individual houses. These can be still more difficult to identify but if they carry a postmark you can guess that the house is probably in that town, for the local card was either specially commissioned and not on sale at all or it was only offered in that one area. Along with houses, there will be postcards of most prominent buildings in the town or city including churches and schools. For village schools in particular, the children at play or somewhere in the picture will increase its interest. Perhaps the most important buildings in a community were the local railway station, public houses, inns, hotels, and the local post office. You may expect to pay double the price where the postmark is the same as the name of the Post Office and much more if postmen or staff are outside in their uniforms. If the railway has ceased to exist, and the station has changed to another use that will make an original picture of it much more valuable. With the old coaching inns, one showing the coach outside ready to depart would be a fine addition to the collection.

## TYPES OF CARD AND WANTS LISTS

You will be able to obtain all these cards in three basically different styles. The most sought-after is often the real photograph, which usually has a glossy finish but is sometimes matt. The test of a good one is to examine it through a magnifying glass when almost all details and names should be very clear. If they are blurred, the original photograph may be to blame but more often than not, the printing is at fault. Sometimes a photograph was printed many times, and touched up and altered until you would hardly recognise it from the original, with modern trams replacing horse-drawn ones, people in early dress removed and other features altered. More often than not, this type of card was produced by a collotype process in sepia or even black and white. The term 'photo-origin' is often used and can be quite misleading, for some of the most poorly printed cards are of photographic origin but are not worthy of the name. The third type of card is in colour and here again these vary in quality from poor to very fine. You have to make your own decision as to just what you consider acceptable.

Many colour views are by local or national artists whose work may either be almost totally unknown or very famous indeed. Some artists are sought by many collectors and this naturally soon pushes the price up. A little research will not only show you which artists you prefer yourself, but also which ones are associated with your locality.

They may have actually lived in your area or they may have liked its scenery, and their pictures were reproduced on local postcards. Sometimes an artist both lived and worked most of his life in one town or county, and you can build up a comprehensive picture of him, showing changes in his style of painting through the years. If you live in the United States, Canada, Australia or the European continent, you can find out about local artists in the same way.

9

Having decided which area you wish to collect, how can you best make out a list of places for your own guidance and that of dealers whose help you might seek. Two of the best methods are:

(i) To photocopy a local map of the area, marking your boundary clearly upon it.

(ii) List all the towns and villages in alphabetical order so that when a dealer sees a card he thinks may be of interest to you he can quickly check the name. A Gazetteer can often be of assistance here and you should be able to find one in your local library. One that omits very few place names in the British Isles is Bartholomew's Gazetteer, which has seen many editions through the years. The more you can define exactly what you want, the better your results are likely to be.

A note of caution is in order here. Having sent a dealer your Wants List you should be in a position to accept a reasonable proportion of the cards he has set aside for you or especially searched out. Although they may be sent on approval, if you send most of them back after he closely followed your requirements (assuming prices were reasonable), you will be unlikely to receive another consignment. But perhaps you will say you already have a large collection and you didn't want to buy duplicates. That is right, but it means you must define your requirements much more precisely or find some other local collectors with whom you can share any approvals, taking the few you need, but selling many of the others elsewhere before returning the few remaining. If you tell him about this arrangement, a dealer will usually extend slightly his approval period.

When your collection is really large, there is no substitute for your own personal search, and a well organised master list of what you have already.

# 3 Everyday Life and Events

In the last chapter we particularly considered *where* people lived. Now we want to consider *how* people lived and what they did. Once again it can be safely said that if a good photographer was active in your area, all the principal events occurring would be recorded and published as postcards, often within a few hours or at least by the next day. In a small and closely-knit community all sorts of things we might now consider rather trivial were recorded on the postcard, and in a larger community where more was happening anyway there is often a still wider selection.

Here is a list of some of the events that may have happened in your locality, and you can watch out for some of these:

| | | |
|---|---|---|
| Air shows | Fairs | Openings |
| Anniversaries | Festivals | Pageants |
| Carnivals | Fires | Processions |
| Concerts | Floods | Sports events |
| Dances | Hunts | Strikes |
| Disasters | Markets | Visits by personalities |

Some of these items are already well-documented. For example, a list of pageants is available in some postcard catalogues, although at times these are wrongly grouped with national exhibitions. If a book has been published giving the local history of your town or county, you may be able to find many of these details there. If not, many libraries now have a Local History Department or someone who specialises in it, and they may be able to show you some files of local newspaper cuttings and pictures. You may even find that your local library has a postcard collection, although it may well lack any sort of organisation.

Next consider local industry, for there may be many postcards of factories, all sorts of mines, industrial mills, windmills and watermills, and if it is a seaside town, a fishing industry or busy harbour.

Then there are the community services, the local police station or fire station with perhaps pictures of a horse-drawn fire-engine and crew and a later motor fire-engine. Whilst mentioning local vehicles a point often overlooked by collectors is the early motor car and the specimens of it that can be collected for one's local county or state according to the registration numbers of the vehicles. In Great Britain a little publication entitled *'Where's that car from?'* gives an alphabetical list of all car registration index letters so that you can quickly list the letters covering your town or area. Then there may be a local hospital or prison with views of the interior and the staff or the prisoners out on exercise.

11

# EVERYDAY LIFE

Country life is also represented by every facet that can be imagined. Perhaps the most interesting one features the ancient methods of agriculture used before the modern combine-harvester and similar giant machines. Ploughing and reaping with horse-drawn implements, harvesting with horse-drawn wagons and the colourful if dangerous pitchfork. Very much sought after are the steam-traction engines, busily working alongside hayricks or barns. There are many farm scenes with sheep-shearing, lambing, a milk-maid with her yoke, and champion cows and bulls. There are scenes around the village pond, the blacksmith busy shoeing a horse, the village pump, stocks or whipping post, and a great variety of country craftsmen at work, crofters, thatchers, wheel-makers and the more specialised occupations such as digging peat. Again, many of the best photographs are those taken by anonymous photographers and issued in very limited editions. I have one showing a group of potato pickers in front of their horse and cart, the girls in aprons and shawls, and men with scarves tied round their necks. In the foreground are half a dozen buckets of potatoes, while on the cart stand two of the older women and a man seated on the horse's hind quarters. Although it will never be known where this picture was taken, it is a fine addition to any country-life collection. Another one I prize is a close-up of a family picnic, the men with knives and forks poised as they tackle a piece of pie, while a large hunk of bread balances on a stretched-out leg. The old type picnic basket is in the foreground and the family dog sits up enquiringly in the lap of the one woman in the picture. The men all wear rough clothes with caps pushed back so this is not an Edwardian party but probably a lunch break of three busy farm workers. Quite in contrast, our fifth *illustration* shows a typical country caravan of the period with some elegantly dressed ladies enjoying a cup of afternoon tea. Notice the bow-tie, the lace and long skirts, the vase of flowers on the table and the intricate carvings which decorate the van.

When it comes to town life, there is an abundance of material. One of the longest and most important sets published is by Rotary Photographic Company under the title 'London Life'. It depicts characters and tradesmen of all types and professions and even includes the Suffragettes. Tuck also issued a photographic London Life series as well as some interesting colour ones. Series 1800 painted by Janet Lewis includes The Flower Stall, The Fruit and Vegetable Stall, The Ice-Cream Stall and night-time scenes of a coffee stall, oyster stall and the 'Cheapjack'. Plenty of people are featured in all these scenes. Series 9015 shows an Italian Organ Grinder, a Street Potter at work with an enthralled group of spectators and a Punch and Judy Show in a London park.

C. W. Faulkner's Series 337, painted by Saville Lumley, shows Flower girls in Piccadilly Circus, Feeding the Gulls on the Embankment, a Recruiting Sergeant at Charing Cross, and Horse Riders in Hyde Park's famous Rotten Row. The Photochrom colour series 'London Types' is interesting and not too difficult to find, and Hartmann and Stewart & Woolf also issued coloured series, one of which is entitled 'London Street Cries'. This reminds me of the famous 'Cries of London' series, painted by F. Wheatley (13 cards) which appeared in many different styles and series

*A pleasant Edwardian afternoon tea party in the country.*

*A typical road repair team ready for action.*

*From the London Life series by Tuck (3714).*

*Note the expressions in this serious game of Deck Quoits.*

from various publishers. Another series by G.D. and D. includes a Knives and Scissors Grinder and an old lady making kettle holders. There is a very varied photographic series of London scenes by Judge; a more recent London Life set published by Charles Skilton includes an East End Rag and Bone Man, trundling along on his horse and cart.

Many scenes of provincial town life can also be found, from a set of six local characters in Aberdeen to Mary Kelynack of Newlyn, Cornwall, who walked to London to see the Queen. There are numerous town criers and many editions of the Ripon Hornblower. A particularly interesting scene is shown in our sixth *illustration*—a typical road repair team from Tickhill, Rotherham, Yorkshire. Behind the men with their shovels, brooms and billy-cans, is the horse-drawn tar-sprayer with its decorative iron wheels; the foreman is in the centre holding the spray nozzle.

There is no end to the cards you can find which show what life was like seventy or eighty years ago, even the family portraits, stiff and uninteresting though many of them may be, will quite often provide some interesting sidelights to add to your collection. Amongst the many song cards which were issued there are a number which show scenes reflecting life in those days. For example, in the Shamrock series, 'Only a Penny' reveals a wistful little girl, seated on the steps of a house with iron railings, offering boxes of matches for a penny each. At her side is a little bundle tied up in a handkerchief. Bamforths also issued a life model series, with many

*Donkeys go best loaded–with space for message on right.*

*Italian Bread Peddlars–A 'Detroit' PMC card No. 5690.*

*A 'Roll Along' Covered Wagon 'out West' in rural Kington, Herefordshire!*

**The Bystander** *Stall at Henley Regatta 1908.*

typical scenes, including the dirty rough little child offering wax lights to passers-by. These children were usually relatives of the Bamforth family.

In the United States, a fine series depicting scenes of every-day life was issued by Detroit Photographic Co. In colour, they include Italian Bread Peddlers, an Organ Grinder, a Chestnut Stand, a Sidewalk Haberdashery, a Telescope Man, and a Banana Cart. The donkey is prominent on many 'Detroits' as they are called. For example, 'A Rocky Mountain Freight Train' is simply a line of mules and donkeys, each with a long wooden board strapped on either side of it. Another, well loaded with wheelbarrow and tools, stands on a ratchet railroad displaying the sign, 'I helped Build Pike's Peak Railway' (near Colorado Springs in the Rocky Mountains). My favourite is a similar card *(illustrated)*, entitled 'The Prospector's Automobile'.

With a keen eye and a little searching, a rich and varied collection can be built up around the everyday life and events at the turn of the century. The happy carefree years before World War I changed everything can come to life, and the entire history of an area can be traced from the picture postcards which so faithfully recorded it.

14

# 4     Early Postcards

Before we consider the many types of subject postcard available, this will be an appropriate point at which to pause and briefly look at the story of the postcard. In looking at its development we can also consider cards of the early period in some detail.

There is no more difficult problem in the history of cartology than the question of its origin. Particularly difficult is the definition which we attach to the word 'postcard' or 'post card'. Then we have to decide when the first pictures appeared, and even what actually constituted a picture.

Part of the reason for this is that long before the postcard was thought of there existed a wide variety of pictorial stationery. When the first postage stamps in the world were introduced in England in 1840 it sparked off a revolution in everything connected with the post. William Mulready quickly designed a pictorial envelope which not only aroused much controversy, but was followed by numerous caricatures as well as others of a more serious nature designed to further various causes. Throughout the nineteenth century it remained fairly popular in both Britain and the U.S.A., but it was finally overtaken by the picture postcard.

At the same time, pictorial notepaper also became popular. This was not the type often seen today, carrying just a small picture, but sometimes it was a large engraving filling the entire top section of the paper. Often these views could also be obtained on stiffer card, and there is no doubt that at times some of these were sent through the post without a cover, and although there were no regulations framed to permit this officially, a small number were bound to slip through in various places.

It has been claimed that some of these private cards constitute the first picture postcard, and that their printer or publisher was the inventor of the idea. This is where the definition becomes so important. To send something through the post it had to conform to the requirements of the postal authorities, and be sent with their official blessing. A freak would not meet this test, any more than a Cinderella stamp receiving a postmark upon it would thereby become a duly authorised postage stamp.

## THE FIRST POST CARD

Considering all the candidates put forward as 'firsts', the Lipman Postal Card issued in the United States in 1861 has the best credentials to date. A U.S. Act of 27th February, 1861 stated, "That cards, blank or printed . . . shall be charged with postage at the rate of 1 cent per ounce, or fraction thereof, to any place in the United States under 1,500 miles; over 1,500 miles, 2 cents an ounce or fraction thereof, to be prepaid by postage stamps." The term 'printed' here referred to the addition of advertising matter.

The Lipman Postal Card was first copyrighted by John P. Charlton of Philadelphia on 17th December, 1861, who soon assigned this copyright to H. L. Lipman of Philadelphia. So far, at least four of these cards have been traced, but all are unused. They have a stamp box in the top right corner, and three horizontal lines for the address, and the reverse side is blank. In the top left corner are the words 'Copyright Secured 1861/Lipman's Postal Card—Patent applied for'. A second issue was printed in May, 1872, of which further copies survive.

This card meets the necessary requirements. It conformed with a proper postal act passed by the nation, and it received the proper copyright for the individual issue in the District Court. But it was still essentially a *private* card, without an imprinted stamp.

The first government-sponsored post card was issued by Austria on 1st October, 1869, and many other countries quickly followed suit, including Great Britain in October 1870, and the United States in May 1873. The idea had been suggested first by Dr. Heinrich von Stephan in 1865 at a German postal congress held at Karlsruhe, but was not taken up. In 1869 it was again recommended by Dr. Emanuel Herrmann of Vienna, and this time the Austrian Post Office acted on the suggestion, and issued their first cards carrying an imprinted Austrian stamp. These are often termed in the United States 'government postals', but are more universally known by the name 'postal stationery cards'. Once the Universal Postal Union had been formed in 1874 (at first called the General Postal Union), it helped to promote the international handling of mail, and initiated the simple term 'postcard'.

## THE FIRST PICTURE POSTCARD

Anyone who drew or painted a picture on a properly authorised postcard was producing a picture postcard, and many early designs exist, one of which is *illustrated* with a clear 1880 postmark applied neatly between the heads of the two ladies glowering at each other across the table. But by their very nature each of these is unique, and cannot be possessed by any other collector. So we need to look for cards with a printed picture of some sort which can be clearly dated to a particular time.

Most contenders for the title of 'first' picture postcard come into the period 1870-1873. One of these is *illustrated*, a Christmas postcard which is one of a series published towards the end of 1870 in colour by lithographer John B. Day, Savoy St., Strand, London. The back is a standard postal stationery one with a half-penny imprinted stamp. It may be argued that this is not a true picture, and some have even said that the first true picture postcard would have to carry a picture intended for purposes of pleasure rather than, say, advertisement. But this is not necessary, for many modern picture postcards carry either a pictorial design, or a picture linked with a promotional theme. The other pictorial design issued in 1870 in Britain well illustrates this point, for it shows quite a small line drawing of the Royal Polytechnic, Regent St., London, with a tiny figure sketched on either side, but it is without doubt a picture carried on an authorised postcard. Where the line does need to be drawn is in the case of a mere symbol or decoration such as was carried on the address side of many early postcards. Perhaps it

*A John Day Christmas postcard in colour. published in 1870.*

*A unique hand-painted picture postcard. artist signed in 1880.*

*A rare Court-size greetings card sent to autograph collector W. R. Bray in 1898.*

*Centenary of birth of Dr. von Stephan. who first suggested the post card in Europe.*

is necessary to ask if what is represented does convey a very definite thought to the mind by means of the picture shown. A mere geometric device would just look pretty, but not do that.

There are other contenders in 1870 itself, including some connected with the Franco-Prussian war, and one produced by a printer in Oldenburg, Germany. Perhaps the earliest *view* cards were issued in Zurich in March, 1872, sketched by artist Franz Borich of Nuremberg, Germany was certainly well ahead in its production of picture postcards on a commercial scale, and a number of cards were published from 1872, including a series of Göttingen by H. Lange. From 1873 a much circulated series of several dozen different German views can be found, distinguished by having the picture printed in the top third of each vertical card.

From this early dominance of the market Germany never looked back. Throughout the remainder of the nineteenth century she was always in the forefront for design, printing techniques and circulation. In fact, the popularity of the picture postcard spread like a wave, commencing in Germany, then into France, Italy, Switzerland and the Low Countries, across into England, and finally over to America and Canada, Australia and Japan. A number of years separated the peak of interest in each country, with Germany reaching it by the turn of the century, England by 1905, and America two or three years later.

In 1899 it was possible to find 3,000 different postcard designs covering every subject within one square half-mile of Paris, and a year later a factory in Frankfurt-on-Main, Germany, had 1,200 employees, and was turning out

100 new designs each working day. Such was the desire to enlarge a postcard collection that one German lady wrote her name and address on the border of a 100 mark note, requesting any gentleman who saw it to send her a picture postcard for her collection. She received many cards by this method, until one recipient of the note wrote saying he collected 100 mark notes, and would she add to his collection in the same way!

Germany became so pre-occupied with the picture postcard that the craze was described this way by the *Standard* in 1899, "The travelling Teuton seems to regard it as a solemn duty to distribute them from each stage of his journey, as if he were a runner in a paper-chase. His first care on reaching some place of note is to lay in a stock, and alternate the sipping of beer with the addressing of post cards. Sometimes he may be seen conscientiously devoting to this task the hours of a railway journey. Would-be vendors beset the traveller on the tops of hills, and among the ruins on lowlands, in the hotels, the café, and even the railway train. They are all over the country, from one end of the Fatherland to the other." The writer described its spread to Britain this way, "The illustrated post card craze, like the influenza, has spread to these Islands from the Continent, where it has been raging with considerable severity." A glance at the Appendix to this book will give some idea of the numbers of cards passing through the post, and it gives consideration to the important question of how many of these cards survive today.

## TYPES OF EARLY CARDS

If you particularly wish to collect early cards, what should you look for? If you just want a colourful collection then the German Gruss aus (Greetings from) multi-view cards will certainly give you that. During the 1890s printing beautiful chromo-lithographs from stone reached its perfection, and the design and layout of many of these cards is superb. A vast number were issued, especially during the years 1897–1900, and the collector needs to distinguish the common ones from the range of scarcer issues. Contrary to the belief of many cartologists, the postmark makes little difference to the value for these years. Only dates before 1897 begin to add to the value.

You can often tell a card from a still earlier period because the colours are lacking and sepia tones predominate. The pictures tend to be either sketches or engravings, and on closer examination are made up of a number of lines. Sometimes a date is given in the design, but the postmark becomes more and more important each year you go back. Here too, cards from countries that did not issue so many postcards are more sought after, and the German colonies are much to be preferred to those of Germany itself. Limited numbers of the Gruss aus style can be found for far-flung spots like China and Ceylon, but the full-size ones are not often found for places in Britain. The London one *illustrated* is very scarce, and you are more likely to locate Scottish places such as Edinburgh, Ayr or Oban.

If you want to collect early Art cards, or social history types, you can find these among French issues, and there are a good number of delightful continental exhibition cards, along with some fine American ones for the 1893 World Columbian Exposition. Early commemorative cards

18

*25th Anniversary of Liberation of Rome, 1895, with papal Cinderella stamp affixed on left.*

*A slightly oversize Irish Court card!*

*A scarce Gruss aus type for London, full size chromo.*

*A chromo PMC for Colorado, U.S.A., in early style.*

command high prices, depending on the particular event, and Russian and Eastern European countries generally are always in demand.

When it comes to cards of Great Britain, it is unusual to find many before 1894, when in September of that year the private picture post card was officially permitted. Prior to that date, most of them are on postal stationery cards, and consist of a few exhibition cards in the early 1890s, and some advertising cards. With only a few months of 1894 remaining, those with postmarks for that year are very few, but they gradually increase each year thereafter, and become quite easy to find for 1899. Most are in two sizes, an oblong shape often called 'intermediate size' and measuring 130 x 83 mm, and a squarer type called 'court size' measuring 115 x 89 mm. The court size was widely used from 1895, and is much more popular with collectors today than the intermediate size. Some carry the words 'Court Post Card' on the back. In November 1899 the full-size continental type was permitted, measuring 140 x 89 mm.

In the United States the early picture post card was almost always an advertising one, from the 1870s through into the 1890s. Some have a very small picture, others so large that they are almost view cards. Those with only a trade mark or a monogram do not rate as picture post cards. In the early 1890s the genuine view card began to make its appearance, along with a few subject cards, and all these cards up to 19th May, 1898 are termed 'Pioneer Postcards'. On that date Congress passed an Act which authorised the private postcard, and this came into effect on 1st July. From then until

19

24th December, 1901 all private cards carried the heading 'Private Mailing Card' usually with a reference to the 1898 Act. They are slightly narrower than the European or continental size card, measuring 140 x 83 mm. It is sometimes a moot point as to whether this 3½ year period should be included with the early one, but it is generally excluded, especially as such a large number of cards survive for those years.

## POSTCARD PERIODS

This raises the question of suitably dividing up the history of the postcard into convenient eras or periods. No hard and fast dates can be set, and in any case the situation has to be different for Europe, for Britain, and for the United States. But some distinction is useful, otherwise it would be meaningless to talk here of 'early cards'.

Starting with the cards of Great Britain we can sensibly outline the following postcard periods:

Period 1    1870-1899    — The Early Postcard
Period 2    1900-1918    — The Golden Age of Postcards
Period 3    1919-1939    — The Doldrums
Period 4    1940-1970    — The Gradual Revival
Period 5    1971-today — The Modern Period

We have already seen that the new full-size card was authorised in Britain in November 1899, so the end of that year truly completed the first stages in the evolution of the postcard. For the Continent that date might need to be slightly earlier, and for America it will be May 1898. If we are looking at the *history* of the postcard as distinct from the subject matter depicted, this is the sort of change that does mark off one era from another.

Some have pointed to the entry of the 'divided back' as marking a new period, but this occurred so gradually that it is not as clear a distinction as has sometimes been thought. In Britain it was authorised early in 1902, but the earliest card so far found with a divided back carries a postmark date in August, 1902. Yet in that month, most cards printed for the delayed Coronation of King Edward VII still have undivided backs, and some publishers did not change over to the new style until the Spring of 1903. As Germany did not change until 1905 and the United States until 1907, this is no help for dating periods of postcard history.

From the year 1900 the collecting boom was really on, so the Golden Age had truly arrived, and although it began to fall off just before the First World War, that revived the interest, which continued throughout those years. Some authorities would separate the two World Wars into separate periods of their own, but this tends to give war postcards an artificial prominence, and for the United States their late entry into the First World War would make that period a mere eighteen months long.

Although 1969 saw the anniversary of the Austrian postcard, the Centenary of the Postcard was celebrated in Britain in 1970 with a special issue card, and this neatly divides those four periods into two of roughly 30 years each, and two of roughly 20 years each. As collectors everywhere once again began to think about the humble postcard, neglected for decades, but bouncing back into the public eye in the 1970s, it can really be said that the picture postcard had 'come of age'.

# 5   Advertisements and Exhibitions

The tremendous variety of subjects found on picture postcards knows no bounds. This can be displayed in a collection of colourful advertisement postcards, perhaps better than any other theme. It is difficult for catalogue editors to know whether they should list all advertisements together or whether an advertisement section should be shown in each of the many other subject headings. Since there are so many advertisement cards running into tens of thousands, it is better to sub-divide them according to the main theme of the picture. To appreciate the reasons for this, consider the main types of advertising card, which are:

Educational                        Products
Hotels and Restaurants      Railways
Industrial                            Shipping
Newspapers and Magazines    Theatre and Circus

The picture shown on the card will generally be related to one or other of the above types. Railway and Shipping lines are the easiest examples to think about. The Railway Companies wished to convince the public that their line offered the finest and fastest trains and the best scenery, so they themselves issued sets of cards showing their trains and the places they visited, and the same principle applied to the shipping lines. All these cards are called 'Officials', because they emanated from an official source. We would obviously classify these as part of the transport section and accordingly, they are dealt with in chapter eleven. Similarly, there are Hotel and Restaurant Officials.

The situation is a little different for Theatre advertisements. These cards were often issued by a promotional agent, but because the pictures relate to the theatre or circus, they are correctly classified under that heading and dealt with in chapter nine.

The principal area of advertising which remains is for the many thousands of products on the market. This is the pure type of commercial advertising. Nevertheless, another subject may still dominate for one reason or another. For example, a famous set of four postcards advertising Birds' Custard Powder was published for the Coronation of Edward VII in 1902. These are correctly classified as Royalty cards, and most collectors of that theme would seek to include these if possible.

So the collector of advertisement postcards has to define the boundaries of his collection. You may want to find just one card advertising each kind of product or you may decide to choose one theme and develop this in all its aspects. For example, a collection of tea cards could include the advertisements for all the different brands, the pictures of tea estates in different countries, the warehouses and factories where the tea is blended and close-up pictures of shops with tea displays in their windows. Most of these cards would be advertisement ones, including those of the Lipton tea estates, but there are many non-advertisement cards showing the tea-pickers at work and the shipping and transport processes.

Advertisement postcards are further divided into poster and semi-poster types, reverse advertisements and inserts and these terms are defined in Appendix 2. Of these the full poster is the most interesting and expensive. It represents in miniature an original poster with its large and ornate lettering which might have been seen on one of the thousands of hoardings throughout the world. Very often these were just the blank walls at the end of a row of terraced houses on the corner of a busy street and they became very untidy at times, but a beautifully designed and coloured poster card looks very fine on the album page. The following is a selected list of some of those available along with the product advertised:

As You Like It Flour
Barber's Linen Thread
Beecham's Pills
Beehive Knitting Wools
Burgess 'M.M.' Pickle
Campbell's Soups
Camp Coffee
Carnation Milk
Champion's Vinegar
Chanteclair Embrocation
C.W.S. Pelaw Polish
Eiffel Hosiery
Erasmic Soap
Firestone Tyres
Fry's Cocoa/Chocolate
Fussell's Milk
Gillette Safety Razors
Gossage's Soap
Grimble's Malt Vinegar
Heinz '57' Varieties
Hill's Biscuits
Horniman's Tea
Hudson's Soap
John Line's Wallpapers
Keiller's Jams

Kellogg's Corn Flakes
Le Page's Liquid Glue
Mazawattee Cocoa/Tea
Mazda Lamps
Morrell's Hams & Bacons
Mustard Horse Nails
Nestle's Milk
New Home Sewing Machines
Old Abbey Whisky
Osram Lamps
Palmer Tyres
Pascall's Sweets
Ripolin Paints
Sandford's Ginger
Schweppe's Table Waters
Shinette Boot Polish
Tosca Thread
Tower Tea
Van Houten Cocoa
Viscan Pet Foods
Walker's Lager Beer/Ales
Whitbread Stout and Ales
Wildspur Yarn
Wrights' Gas Cookers
Yorkshire Relish

Because a particular poster card exists does not always mean that the corresponding actual full-size poster was used originally. Some were designed solely to be issued as picture postcards. An extremely interesting collection can be made by combining street scenes showing actual advertisement sites with a sample of each of the poster postcards. Difficult though this is, it adds the real-life dimension which turns a mere assemblage into something very individual.

Most poster cards were published by the commercial companies themselves, many of them in sets. Some series were also issued by ordinary postcard publishers. The best of these is without doubt the Tuck 'Celebrated

An early American p.s. Advertisement, postmarked 1890.

A typical example of a full-out Poster Advertisement.

Another poster type with added transport interest.

Tuck's became sole British agents for this American printing firm long before postcards were thought of in Raphael House.

Posters', with more than sixty cards, followed by 'Famous Posters in Miniature' from Henry Moss and Company, and C. W. Faulkner's Series 'Famous Showcards'.

There are many other non-poster advertisement cards for a great variety of products, some of which were given away with a packet or tin or could be sent for by means of a coupon for a few pence. Others were just view cards with a single catch line on the back advertising the product, but plenty of them have some connection with the product itself, such as the Lemco Cattle Studies, Hartley's Jam Preparation, or Chivers' English Fruit Studies.

Magazines published at the time often gave away sets of free postcards and some were linked with special offers. Many of these were poorly printed and not worth the interest of the serious collector. But some are of much better quality, including an interesting rural series free with the weekly *Tale-Teller* and a sporting series for the *Owl*. Some of these cards are also very scarce, such as the 'Family Herald' series, and the excellent series of Comic Write-aways issued by the *Globe*. A much sought-after series was issued by the *Racing Pigeon* which depicts close-ups of winners for various years and events.

Cards were used to advertise new magazine serials to encourage a greater readership. *The Boys' Leader* ran a series 'The Adventures of Sunny Jim and Dismal David', with a short note from the editor underneath, while two kittens encourage one to always read the *Childrens' Friend*. There are a number of poster adverts, the easiest to find being one for *Tit-Bits* with a boy so engrossed in it he doesn't notice the cat eating the fish he should be delivering. There are some fine posters for *Lloyds News* and *Answers*, and

23

one of a train speeding through the night tells you it is 'Bringing You the *London Daily Mail* at sixty miles an hour—one halfpenny everywhere'. Front pages of newspapers often appear on postcards, most common of which are several different issues of the *Military Mail*. Another series issued by Hills of Sunderland includes many local papers, like the *Kelso Chronicle*. There are a number of continental series, some including specialist newspapers like the *Nouvelliste Vaudois* of Lausanne. A picture of a child reading the *Cleveland Plain Dealer* proclaims that no breakfast is complete without one. A coupon cut from the newspaper would obtain one postcard from a set of sixteen.

There are many comic cards which show folded newspapers with quite genuine readable dates and articles, illustrating an awkwardly worded classified advertisement. Two of the most notable series of these were 'Addled Ads' and 'Agony Column', published by Misch and Company.

## EXHIBITIONS

The large commercial exhibitions are closely tied in with advertising and so it is appropriate to consider these here as well. Most major exhibitions held this century have been included on picture postcards though modern issues tend to be fairly limited. For some, notably the Franco-British Exhibition in 1908 at the White City, London, and the World's Fair in 1904 at St. Louis in the United States, the total number of cards issued was enormous. It is a relatively simple matter to build a collection of ordinary issues of most of these exhibitions at reasonable cost. But there are many special issues featuring particular stands or special exhibits and these are not easy to find.

Once again, a special theme may be preferred such as that of the Entente Cordiale, which was the theme for the Franco-British Exhibition. A series of comic cards issued by Millar and Lang carried the title in large letters flanked by the English and French flags. The comic pictures were accompanied by captions in both languages (National Series 677).

A Valentine series includes a close-up of a motor car decorated with English and French flags, driven by John Bull with his French counterpart gesticulating towards the Exhibition buildings while a bull-dog and a French poodle are on top of the open rear seat. Another card stresses unity, with the lands of Britain and France only divided by the narrow English Channel which is effectively bridged by Britannia and a French girl crossing huge and colourful flags. The theme can be extended well beyond the exhibition itself by adding, for example, a series of cards recording Edward VII's visit to France in May 1903 and the return visit of President Emile Loubert as commemorated by the Dover Standard's card of 6th July that same year.

Some of the nicest cards available relate to the early continental exhibitions held during the 1890s. These are often Gruss aus types (see Appendix 2 on Definitions) and are fine multi-view chromo-lithographs. Those with the special exhibition postmark usually cost more than unused ones. For the Paris exhibition of 1900, there is an amazing selection of cards available, with or without advertising overprints and including many which when held up to the light reveal either brilliant colouring, additional

*Example of a semi-poster, without display-type lettering, a superb American chromo with reverse advertisement in picture-form.*

*A combination poster advertisement with railway and shipping, map and windmill interest, set in an Art Nouveau frame.*

*A comic exhibition card in poster form.*

*A Tuck Paris 1900 Exhibition card, from a fine chromo set of 12.*

*A popular theme, archery and rifle contests, with special Festival postmark.*

pictures or advertisements. One of the very best sets is the Tuck 'Paris Exhibition' series of twelve cards (individually numbered 746–757) with superbly designed multi-vignettes, of which number 755 is *illustrated*.

In Scotland, some excellent cards were produced for the Glasgow Exhibition of 1901, including a set of artistic scenes by the Belgian landscape painter Henri Cassiers. In America a fine series of cards was issued for the Columbian Exhibition in Chicago in 1893. The World's Fair held in St. Louis in 1904, the Jamestown Tercentennial Exposition in 1907, the Alaska-Yukon Exposition in 1909, and the Panama-Pacific Exposition in 1915 are all noteworthy for a number of excellent sets.

Because most exhibitions included special displays, these should not be overlooked by collectors of other themes. Those interested in Japanese cards can find much material from the Japan-British Exhibition of 1910. Several exhibitions included American Indians and scenes from the Wild West, and Russian types were also popular.

The scope offered by advertising and exhibition postcards is very extensive indeed, and with a little ingenuity a wide variety of themes can be developed.

# 6   Art and Artists

When we think of art on postcards we are quite likely to imagine those rather dull productions which can be obtained from most art galleries and museums. But some of the most beautifully designed and expensive postcards that can be purchased today are those classified under the headings of 'Art Nouveau' and 'Art Deco'.

Art Nouveau, or the New Art, was the modern style of free art which sprang up on the continent and especially in France and the Low Countries during the last few years of the 19th century. In a sense it was a protest against all that had gone before, and an endeavour to reach new heights by finding a style that could be applied to all fine arts and crafts whether exterior or interior. Its outstanding characteristic was the use of linear patterns based on natural shapes, especially those of flowers and plants. Lines were flowing, curving and continually interlaced and intertwined.

Because the postcard was rising in popularity at an exactly parallel time to the flowering of Art Nouveau, it was natural that this new medium should be used by the New Art. Perhaps the most celebrated Art Nouveau postcard artist was the Czech-born Alphonse Mucha and for some years past his splendid postcards have made the top individual prices at many auctions. You may only be able to admire these from a distance but there are many other similar artists whose work is not nearly as expensive and a list of these follows, with the most popular and costly labelled as category A, those in the middle range as category B and the less sought after artists as category C:

| | | | |
|---|---|---|---|
| Arpad, Basch | A | MacDonald, A. K. | C |
| Berthon, Paul | A | Martini, Alberto | B |
| Bilibene, Ivan | B | Mataloni, Giovanni | C |
| Christiansen, Hans | A | Metlicovitz, Leopoldo | C |
| Combaz, Gisbert | A | Meunier, Henri | A |
| Daniell, Eva | B | Mignot, Victor | C |
| Döcker, E. Jnr. | C | Moser, Kolomon | B |
| Hohenstein, Adolfs | C | Mucha, Alphonse | A |
| Jozsa, Carl | B | Noury, Gaston | B |
| Lelee, Leopold | C | Schmucker, Samuel L. | B |
| Kirchner, Raphael | A | Steinlen, Alexandre | A |

This is only an approximate guide for tastes can change and an almost unknown artist can suddenly rise in popularity or a great quantity of cards can be found to exist for one of the more popular artists and collectors will avoid them.

Besides those cards entirely devoted to Art Nouveau designs, there are many others where the subject matter is set within an art nouveau border or there will be embellishments in this style. Because these frequently go unrecognised, they are missed by many collectors, so you do not have to have a large purse in order to make a representative selection of this art style.

Art Deco burst suddenly into prominence during the 1920s although it had earlier origins. In many respects it is a style less easy to define than that of Art Nouveau for it employed a series of opposites in jagged lines, dots and checks, ballooning dresses and often bright slabs of colour. It was a medium appropriate to children's and greeting postcards, although the more expensive types are usually glamorous subjects. Once again, we can divide Art Deco artists into the same three categories used for Art Nouveau:

| | | | |
|---|---|---|---|
| Brunelleschi | A | Mercer, Joyce | C |
| Chiostri | B | Montedoro, M. | A |
| Cremer, Rie | B | Nashnyekov | B |
| French, Annie | A | Scattina | B |
| Grosze, Manni | C | Shand, C. E. | B |
| Harbour, Jennie | C | Smith, Jessie Wilcox | A |
| Hartridge, Norman | C | Wanke, Alice | A |
| Koehler, Mela | A | Wennerberg, B. | B |
| Longley, Chilton | B | | |

Illuminated art is an interesting aspect at present somewhat neglected. This mediaeval form of decoration is usually found on Italian postcards. The best ones are those published by E. Sborgi. They are richly coloured and frequently gilded and embossed. There are illuminated initials and pictures liberally sprinkled with heraldic emblems.

An outstanding series depicting the entire line of Popes was published by L. Ferloni, Rome and consists of 264 cards which can be obtained with the inscriptions in eight different languages. When Pius the tenth became Pontiff in 1903, a final unnumbered card was added to complete this beautiful chromo-lithograph series.

It is possible to make a very large collection of the world's most famous paintings. The cartologist is well advised to avoid the many sepia productions and to seek those which most nearly approach the originals in colour and effect. The World's Galleries series issued by Stengel of Dresden is one of the very best, beautifully printed and on good stout board.

## LANDSCAPE AND MARINE ARTISTS

This is one of the largest fields for the postcard collector, for the work of literally thousands of artists can be found. Very frequently this is the only record of many of their pictures, for they were painted especially for the postcard medium. Some of these artists are famous, and their original pictures fetch large sums at auction and can often be seen in art galleries. But for every artist like this, there are ten more who are practically unknown. So it is good to take a careful look at many of these and pick out one or two that you like, for you can then form a collection at minimum cost without too much competition. You could even build up your own checklist of cards and find out something about the artist and so help to put him on the map. You may also wish to collect the work of an artist who painted in your particular neighbourhood. Or you may want to develop a special subject from a variety of artists, and marine paintings offer much that is interesting here.

In addition to postcards with the artist's signature or initials, one should not ignore those that are unsigned, just because it happens that some postcard publishers preserved the anonymity of their artists. Many of these are now being identified and we can expect this to continue as research proceeds.

## STILL LIFE, ANIMALS AND CHILDREN

If you prefer still life subjects or figures, there is a wide choice once again. There are some very beautiful floral cards, many of them embossed chromos and again, it is best to select those where the picture is most realistically reproduced. Among the artists most sought here are C. Klein, M. Billing and R. A. Foster.

There are many animal, figure, portrait, genre and sporting scenes, and Dutch and Japanese subjects were very popular. The following list gives some of these artists and the subjects they excelled in:

| | | | |
|---|---|---|---|
| Aldin, Cecil C. | animals | Laporte | genre |
| Anders, O. | animals | Lester, Adrienne | animals |
| Barnes, A. E. | animals | Lewin, F. G. | Dutch |
| Baumgarten, Fritz | genre | Lewis, Janet | genre |
| Bebb, Minnie Rosa | animals | Linsdell, Leonard | genre |
| Beecroft, Herbert | sporting | Linzell, Ernest | sporting |
| Billinge, Ophelia | animals | Lumley, A. Saville | genre |
| Bormeister, R. | genre | Lynde, Raymond | fig./portrait |
| Carey, J. | genre | MacDonald, A. K. | Dutch |
| Cassiers, Henri | Dutch | Maguire, Helena | animals |
| Chatterton, F. J. S. | birds | Menpes, Mortimer | figure/genre |
| Cheney, Leo | Dutch | Müller, August | animals |
| Cheviot, Lillian | animals | Pope, Dorothy T. | animals |
| Cobbe, Bernard | animals | Rankin, George | birds |
| Colby, V. | animals | Reichert, C. | animals |
| Drummond, Norah | animals | Sauber, Robert | genre |
| Fagan, G. W. | genre | Schonian, Alfred | animals |
| Gear, Mabel | animals | Scrivener, Maude | animals |
| Gerstenhauer, J. G. | Dutch | Sharbina, Prof. F. | Russia |
| Green, Roland | birds | Stokes, G. Vernon | animals |
| Greenbank, A. | sporting | Tarrant, Percy | figure |
| Griset, Ernest | figure/genre | Theile, Arthur | animals |
| Hammond, Gertrude D. | figure | Thorburn, Archibald | birds |
| Hardy, E. Stuart | Japanese | Valter, Eugenie M. | animals |
| Heyermans, Jean A. | figure | Valter, Florence E. | animals |
| Jalland, G. H. | figure/sporting | Valter Frederick E. | animals |
| Jungman, Nico W. | figure | Veit, M. | animals |
| Kennedy, A. E. | animals | Velten, W. | animals |
| Kipper, L. J. | animals | Whishaw, M. C. | figure/genre |
| Lancaster, Percy | figure | Wright, George | animals/sport. |

28

Mushroom children, a popular subject in the United States.

A delightful C. Klein chromo from the scarce flower alphabet.

An arresting portrait set against a Basque background.

A superb Art Nouveau type chromo poster advertisement by A. Terzi.

A card from artist Parsons Norman giving his Studio address in Suffolk.

A typical glamour study by M. Cherubini.

A hand-painted caricature of professional quality.

When the fashion in hats threatened to blot out everything else!

The field of children's cards is immense, some of the most attractive being the early chromo undivided backs. The individual picture can often make quite a difference to the price here depending on whether dolls, gollywogs, teddy-bears or other toys are prominently included. Our list of children's artists once again makes use of the same three categories, A, B, C:

| | | | | | | | |
|---|---|---|---|---|---|---|---|
| Anderson, V. G. | B | Frank, E. | C | Parkinson, Ethel | A |
| Attwell, Mabel, L. | A | Gassaway, Katherine | A | Paterson, Vera | B |
| Averill, Joyce | B | Goodman, Maude | A | Petersen, Hannes | B |
| Barber, C. W. | B | Guttmann, Bessie P. | A | Phlo | B |
| Barham, Sybil | A | Gozzard, F. W. | B | Preston, Chloe | B |
| Bertiglia, A. | B | Hardy, Florence | A | Richards, Eugenie | B |
| Birch, Nora A. | C | Hartridge, Norman | B | Richardson, Agnes | A |
| Bowley, A. L. | B | Hodge, Valerie | C | Rose, Freda Mabel | B |
| Brisley, E. C. | B | Horsfall, Mary | B | Right | B |
| Brisley, Nina | B | Hudson, Isabel | C | Sandford, H. Dix | A |
| Brundage, Frances | A | Jacobs, Helen | B | Sherborne, M. | C |
| Busi, A. | C | James, Ivy Millicent | A | Sigsbeeker, Mary | B |
| Caldecott, Randolph | B | Jenkins, Blanche | B | Smith, Jessie Wilcox | A |
| Clapsaddle, Ellen H. | A | Griggs, H. B. | B | Sowerby, Millicent | A |
| Cloke, Rene | B | Guarino, Anthony | B | Stanton, C. R. | B |
| Cooper, Phyllis | C | Lambert, H. G. C. Marsh | A | Symonds, Constance | B |
| Cowham, Hilda C. | C | Little Pitche | B | Tarrant, Margaret | A |
| Cownie, Florence | C | Kermer, A. | C | Tempest, D. | B |
| Dean, Dora | B | Mair, Willebeek le | A | Twelvetrees, C. H. | A |
| Dexter, Marjorie M. | B | Mallet, Beatrice | C | Upton, Florence | A |
| Duddle, Josephine M. | B | Margetson, Hester | B | Wall, Bernard | A |
| Dewees, Ethel H. | B | Miller, Hilda T. | B | Wanke, Alice | A |
| Ebner, Pauli | A | Nash, Adrienne A. | B | White, Brian | B |
| Edgerton, Linda | B | Nystrom, Jenny | A | White, Flora | B |
| Farmer, Clement | B | O'Neill, Rose | A | Wiederseim, Grace G. | A |
| Feiertag, K. | A | Outcault, Richard F. | A | Wilcocks, A. M. | C |
| Fialkowska, W. | A | Outhwaite, Ida Rentoul | A | Williams, Madge | C |
| Folkard, Charles | B | Page, Ernest | B | Wuyts, A. | B |
| Forres, Kit | C | Palmer, Phyllis, M. | C | | |

## GLAMOUR AND FASHION

The final group of artists' cards come under the heading of glamour. Beautiful girls are a natural subject for the picture postcard and they may vary from the erotic to the over-dressed fashion model. It is a very individual field where the artist who pleases one person will be shunned by another and the great variety available makes it certain that you will find some to please you if you wish to collect this subject. After some years in the doldrums, there is a revival of interest in glamour.

One most interesting aspect of Glamour still remains to be discovered by most postcard collectors—the development of fashion. Not only can the history of fashion be traced through the centuries with the aid of such sets as 'Palais du Costume' published by Lemercier of Paris, but companies such as the Fitzall Bandeau Company issued their own postcards to promote their glorious productions. One could just make a collection of huge hats alone, many of them with a touch of fantasy as one tries to find the diminutive lady quite lost 'neath the latest creation. The craze over the harem skirt also produced enough cards to form quite a collection. A Valentine set portrays the effect of this new acquisition:

"Since Mary's got a harem skirt
And given up the hobble,
She now can catch a motor-bus,
And you should see her toddle."

Many cards give a date for the fashion displayed, as for example, the card drawn by Xavier Sager 'La Mode en 1918—Coiffure Chantecler'. Even the men do not escape as shown by the Valentine series 'Coming modes for men or what will it end in'.

So the artist field holds great potential for the budding postcard collector, or as a means of extending existing collections. Even if the theme you choose is quite a narrow one, you can be certain that with a little patient searching you will find more cards than you thought could possibly exist.

My final suggestion concerns a type of card much neglected and sometimes despised at present. It is the hand-painted artist card, and although some of these are the work of poor amateurs there are many excellent and very professional cards. Certain publishers produced 'hand-painted' sets and these are very fine, but the genuine one-off production we are talking about here is painted on a card from a packet of plain ones which could be purchased at any stationer's shop. The *illustration* is one of several drawn by Will Hayden and the faces are all just as full of expression as is this one. You can be sure of one thing in making a collection such as this, you not only have the originals but no other cartologist in the world possesses the same cards.

# 7   Comic and Fantasy

The artist drawn card finds a quite different expression in the field of comic and humour. There is also a great variation in the quality of the humour which so far as the picture postcard is concerned, has tended to deteriorate the nearer it comes to the present day. But, considering the nature of Edwardian times, some examples are not so veiled as we might expect them to be. These cards were usually anonymous and unless the theme is of particular interest, they don't match the popularity of the signed cards. So, as in earlier lists, the letters A, B & C give an approximate guide to the most popular artists, the middle range and the least sought after:

| | | | | | |
|---|---|---|---|---|---|
| Adams, B. | B | Fleury, Hermann | B | Owen, Will | B |
| Aldin, Cecil † | A | Fuller, Edmund G | B | Parlett, Harry | B |
| Aris, A. | B | Fyfe, Clement | B | Payne, G. M. | B |
| Aris, E. | B | Gilson T/Ludgate | B | Penny, Theo. | C |
| Bairnsfather, Bruce | B | Graeff | C | Pirkis, Albert G. | B |
| Barnes, G. L. † | B | Greenall, Jack | B | Pyp | B |
| Biggar, J. L. | C | Grimes | B | Quinton, Harry | C |
| Boulanger, Maurice † | B | Hardy, Dudley | A | Roberts, Violet † | A |
| Bradshaw, Percy V. | A | Hassall, John | A | Robinson, W. Heath | A |
| Browne, Tom | A | Henley, Percy A. | C | Rowntree, Harry | B |
| Buchanan, Fred | B | Hill, Raven | A | Sandford, H. Dix | B |
| Bull, Rene | A | Hilton, Alf. | B | Schonflug, F. | A |
| Buxton, Dudley | B | Hurst, Hal | B | Shaw, W. Stocker | C |
| Carter, Reg. | A | Hyde, Graham | B | Shepheard, G. E. | A |
| Carter, Sidney | B | Kinsella, E. P. | A | Smith, Syd. | C |
| Christie, G. F. | B | Leete, Alfred | B | Spatz (Fred Gothard) | B |
| Colbourne, Lawrence | B | Lewin, F. G. | B | Spurgin, Fred (F.S.) | A |
| Comicus | C | Ludovici, A. | A | Stampa, G. L. | B |
| Crow | B | Luke, William | C | Studdy, George E. | A |
| Crombie, C. M. | B | McGill, Donald | A | Syd | C |
| Cynicus (M. Anderson) | A | Mackain, F. | B | Thackeray, Lance | A |
| Davey, George | B | Mason, Finch | B | Theile, Arthur † | A |
| Donadini Jnr. | B | Maurice, Reginald | B | Thomas, Bert | B |
| Duncan, J. A. (Hamish) | B | May Phil. | A | Wain, Louis † | A |
| Dwiggins, C. V. (Dwig) | B | Meggendorfer, Lothar | A | Ward, Dudley | B |
| Earnshaw, H. C. | B | Moreland, Arthur | A | Wood, Lawson | A |
| Ellam, William, H. | A | Morgan, F. E. | C | | |

†These artists usually depict comic dressed animals in human situations.

It should not be concluded from the above list that those cards in brackets 'B' and 'C' are of little interest. Many very well-drawn cards have not been brought to the attention of postcard collectors generally and so they still wait to be 'discovered'. It is also true that whereas some artists, such as Donald McGill, had thousands of cards published over a long period of years, others may have had less than a hundred issued by just one publisher. Examples of out of the way artists on Tuck cards alone are George Cruikshank (some fine chromo undivided backs) Hubert Whatley and 'Poy' (Percy Fearon). Even a fine artist such as G. H. Jalland is almost totally ignored despite the fact that the Fine Arts Society exhibited many of his paintings. It is difficult to understand why some artists have so far been omitted from the postcard catalogues, for it cannot be that the editors have never seen their cards.

It is fairly simple to build a comic collection around a particular theme and there are also certain catchphrases which form a good basis for one. 'When Father says "Turn"', was invariably linked with the large family that all shared one bed; 'Is marriage a failure' highlighted the henpecked husband; 'My Word! if . . . ' was the preface to any number of phrases with perhaps the most popular one being 'My Word, If I Catch You Bending'.

Comic cards capture the new 'crazes' which hit the populace from time to time. From 1901 to 1903 it was Ping-Pong, Diabolo or the 'Devil-on-two-sticks' in 1907, and roller skating in 1909. Of these we may be least familiar with Diabolo which may owe its name to the exclamation Diablo, Ho! drawn from Iago in Shakespeare's Othello, Act II, Scene III. A wooden 'Cottonreel' was tossed and balanced on a string attached to two sticks held in the hands. The effect of this craze is well demonstrated in a Bamforth comic card showing four boys on the steps of their friends' house; 'Can Tom go with us to Sunday School?' is the caption, but held behind each boy's back and invisible to the lady at the door, is a pair of Diabolo sticks.

Not quite so easy to find are the more local comic cards. This doesn't refer to those cards that merely have the name of a particular town or seaside resort on them—a device used by many publishers to help the sale of their cards. Rather the theme itself is a local one. For example, the comment of a Lancashire Mill lad, 'Yes dear, by rights I *am* the Duke of Portland'. The

*Much sought after series by Valentine, Snow White and the Seven Dwarfs.*

*When the English language just proves too much for people, and they often go off their head!*

*A very scarce Tuck series with fantasy heads, 'Our Boy Scouts' (9950).*

*A Tom Browne original in colour wash on art board, for the American market. (DB 2621).*

*A typical fantasy type—when the cooks are away, everything in the kitchen can play.*

moon smiles disbelievingly and beneath the shuttlecock emblem in the top left hand corner is a pair of boots with the words 'My Word, if you're not off'. Some of these local cards poke fun at real happenings in the community, so, when a new bye-law was passed at Eastbourne prohibiting barking on the beach, the Mayor and the Police are seen keeping watch on a tiny little dog at the end of a breakwater, and below is the ditty:

"Unhappy dog! here comes the Mayor in state,
One little bark—and sad will be thy fate!"

A World War 1 card drawn by Alfred Leete depicts a sensation in Weston-super-Mare. 'Startling discovery of a German about to shell Madeira Cove and neighbourhood'. Everyone is trailing him, soldiers, boy scouts and the local reporter.

Some outstanding comic collections include two by Tuck, 'Jokes from Punch' and 'American Humor from "Puck"'. Wrench also produced a long series of Punch cards, many of them on the popular theme of the Prehistoric. Some later Tuck series of the nineteen-thirties and World War II are 'Useless Eustace' by Jack Greenall, reproduced from the *Daily Mirror*; 'An ITMA Wisecrack', and 'All My Own Work by Grimes' from the *Star*. Valentine produced the ever popular 'Bonzo' series of the adventures of a comic dog by George Studdy, and the 'Nipper' series by Brian White from the *Daily Mail*. There is also a long American series relating the events in the life of 'Private Breger'.

## FANTASY CARDS

Another aspect of comicality is found in the fantasy card, which can be defined as any picture drawn from the imagination rather than real life. Most popular and expensive are the fantasy heads which can be divided into two basic types. There are those where the head is formed from a number of beautiful girls all lying at different angles or in contorted shapes. The second type has a normal picture, often of two people at a table, where the background is so arranged that at a distance it gives the impression of a huge skull. Almost as expensive are the mountain faces where figures and faces make up the mountain peaks, especially the Alps. Map faces are also popular where islands and coastlines are slightly adjusted to form, for example, Miss Atlantic kissing Miss Pacific at the Panama Canal.

Multiple babies have lost a little of their earlier popularity, where whole fields of cabbages grew baby heads left, right and centre, or dozens of children pop out of a top hat or a cone of twisted newspaper. Less usual is the bunch of cherries on a leafy twig with a face peeping out from each cherry, and there are cards of humans with animal faces.

You can find Jules Verne airships and all types of objects in the sky. A glamour girl floats on a bottle of stout over Blackpool Pier, a couple with their umbrella up sail over Dresden, and a man drinking beer sits astride a propellor driven sack of hops over Saaz. An early car, much resembling Chitty-Chitty-Bang-Bang floats high over Mulberry Bend Park, New York, its occupants waving to astonished pedestrians getting cricks in their necks. Two boys on a small aeroplane paint the face of the moon while a third climbs up a short ladder to put on his top hat. A peep one hundred years on over Zurich shows the air filled with airships and biplanes, but only the

34

*The category known as 'dressed animals'-another fantasy form; Ullman's 'Kute Kittens' series 118.*

*A modern fantasy card from Switzerland p/Jaeger, 'Cheese-making' by Minouvis No. 47.*

*Well, hello; that's a smart hat you have there!*

hot air balloon and a couple of airships resemble anything that still exists today, never mind in 2010.

There are views of London and Birmingham looking like Venice with gondolas plying the waters of Piccadilly Circus. Not to be forgotten are the strange contraptions of Heath Robinson or the grotesque engines of the Far Tottering and Oyster Creek Railway of the 1951 Festival of Britain. Some modern Swiss cards issued by Jaeger of Geneva depict tiny people having great problems in cheese-making and the Swiss embroidery industry; they are drawn by Minouvis.

Distortion of size provides another collecting theme, usually known as 'Exaggerations'. There are hundreds of American cards with railway trucks carrying outsize vegetables, or farmhands trying to coax along ducks that are twice their own size. Most sought after are the real photo types published by W. H. Martin. There are a number of comic cards where the people have extra large heads and into this category can also be placed those portrait cards which were taken in studios with a prepared backdrop. People put their own heads through a hole above a painted character, and the results are often most amusing.

Dressed animals are also really fantasy cards, although they haven't found their correct place yet in some postcard catalogues. These could form a really large collection if cards are added showing animals engaging in human enterprises. Here dogs try to ride bicycles and one comes a cropper. In a Tuck 'Aeroplanes' series cats steer and balance on early aeroplanes, and the cat and dog academies are very popular. On the Tuck series 'Egg-Cellent', egg-head porters drawn by G. E. Shepheard rush up and down the station platform as the egg-head guard blows his whistle. Nister issued some fine chromo dressed animals and the New York Ullman Company published Kute Kittens.

Fantasy cards are generally more expensive than most ordinary comic types, the exception being those comics signed by top artists, or printed in chromo-lithography. For all these themes there is virtually no 'completion' point, so the collector must firmly define his own boundaries.

# 8   Novelties and Silks

The novelty card is exactly what the name suggests. By some new or novel feature it was designed to catch the attention of a likely purchaser. When the novelty card really became popular the postcard was big business and publishers were trying by every means possible to sell more and more cards. Novelties fall into several main categories:

1. Those made of different materials
2. Those which have materials appliquéd to them
3. Those with mechanical or moveable parts
4. Hold-to-light and luminous cards
5. Composite sets and puzzle cards
6. Various other novelties

1. Almost every type of material has been sent through the mail as a postcard: aluminium, basketry, brown paper, celluloid, leather, panel cards, peat, bronzed tin-plate and wood. Some of these caused trouble with the postal authorities and had to be withdrawn or changed in format. Cards made from peat are so dark that it is difficult to see the picture on them, but a special process was patented which rolled in a thin sheet of white paper capable of taking colour printing. Perhaps the greatest variety of one kind of material is the use of wood and includes balsa wood, bamboo, real tree bark, orange wood from California and some a quarter-of-an-inch thick. There are many kinds of bark, one of maple bark has a Red Indian etched on it in colour, and another is cut from an oak tree planted by Sir Walter Scott around 1815.

2. All kinds of materials have been attached to postcards. Felt (often wrongly described as velvet) was very popular, usually in the shape of all kinds of animals; flower sprays and leaves, some of them dried from places such as Palestine and South Africa; glass eyes; miniature gramophone records that really play a tune on the special little gramophone which was provided; metal models of all kinds, mirrors, shamrock seeds, even little tubes of water-colours, and cigars and cigarettes for which the retailer was required to have a tobacco licence. Birds and hats were made from real feathers, pictures of children had real hair attached and there were all sorts of other substances, including coal, granite and sandpaper. Pictures were made in coloured sand or from genuine bus and tram tickets. One of the most popular types was made by cutting up postage stamps of various colours and countries and attaching these in the form of a pattern. They frequently display great ingenuity and delightful artistry. Spring tails were attached to donkeys and other animals and enclosed in an envelope so that when they were pulled out the tail sprang up to surprise the recipient. Some fine costume studies have skirts and other clothing in appliquéd satin. Many pictures were outlined with an adhesive substance and then sprinkled with tinsel or spangles and even small imitation jewels.

*A clever montage made from French 10c and 25c stamps, face and hands drawn in, then gilded with tinsel (E. 738).*

*Appears luminous in the dark after exposing to a bright light.*

*A 'large letter' alphabet card, a Rotary hand-coloured photograph.*

3.   Under this heading are the many mechanical cards operated by a lever which pushes and pulls part of the design to bring it to life. Some of these are kaleidoscopes passing through a brilliant rainbow of colours. Others have calendars and figures operated by rotating wheels. Some squeak when they are pressed and others can be inflated to form a small ball or model. The transformation card has a flap which alters the picture entirely from the one first seen, others have pop-up figures and some rapidly change the scenes by means of roller blinds. There are moveable hats and paper chains, one of which opens to a length of seven or eight feet. A real fan extends in several sections beyond the card to which it is attached and on another the young lady standing on her bathmat moves a fan up and down to hide her nakedness.

4.   There are several kinds of hold-to-light card. The cut-out type has windows and other lighted areas cut out of the top layer of card, and then a thin sheet of coloured paper is glued between that and the back so that when it is held up to the light the windows appear to glow as if lit up at night, some yellow, some red, some green according to the picture being viewed. The transparency on the other hand has no cut-out parts but allows images or colours to be seen when held to the light which are not apparent in the normal way. Invisible people appear or advertisements are written in the sky, especially in exhibition cards. Because this type is more effective, it is generally more expensive than the cut-out. The final type here is very different. You hold the picture side up to a bright light, then turn all the lights off and the picture of a flower will literally become luminous in the dark. These cards were issued under a special patent by the Luminous Print Company, and they really work very effectively.

5.   Composite sets are made up of a number of cards which when placed in a square or oblong, usually reveal a large superimposed portrait. In the sets of

ten or twelve cards the scenes on each card relate episodes in the story of that person. A similar type normally made up of from three to six cards are known as 'Section Postcards', or 'Installment Sets'. Often of comic and puzzling nature one could be sent each day, thus keeping the recipient guessing as to the final outcome or result until the last card was received. For example, a Wellman series of four cards asks 'Did this—ever—happen—to you?'. On the first card our hero is sitting tight, holding the chair with both hands while one trouser leg disappears off the card to the right in a straight line, the second and third cards merely continue the straight black line right across the card as the message proceeds; the last two words appear on the fourth card and now we see his glamorous lady-love is not just trying to get his shoe off but is stretching him for all she is worth. Animals were popular for this kind of set, particularly the dachshund and the giraffe. On a different theme is the Birmingham Express, with six cards originally joined together to form a complete train of an engine and five carriages. Here is a list of some of these with the number of cards making up the set (C indicates Composites):

| | | | |
|---|---|---|---|
| Alligator | 4 | La Gaite á la Caserne | C. 10 |
| Cat | 5 | Life of Christ | C. 10 & 12 |
| Christmas Tree | 4 | Magpie, The Polite | 3 |
| Dachshund, The Elongated | 4 | Man in Bath with long legs | 3 |
| Dutch Hound, A. | 3 | Map of London | 6 |
| Fish Story | 3 & 4 | Map of Paris | 4 |
| Frog | 3 | Mignon | C. 10 |
| Frog and the Fly | 3 | Missing Link, The | 6 |
| Giant Fish | 3 & 4 | Napoleon (var. sets) | C. 10 & 12 |
| G.P. Government Tea | C. 6 | Pig (1 set by Thiele) | 5 |
| Italian Kingdom's 50th Ann. | C. 10 | Rabbit & the Rhinoceros | 3 |
| Jeanne d'Arc | C. 10 | Santa Claus | 3 & 4 |
| Kaiser's Head | C. 6 | Stork holding baby | 3 |
| Kate Greenaway's April Children | C. 8 | Swan and the child | 3 |
| King Albert of Belgians | C. 8 | Uncle Sam | 4 |
| King Haakon of Norway | C. 8 | Valentine | 4 |
| | | Zouaves | C. 10 |

Many other novelties exist including a number of puzzle cards. There are those where you turn the card around to find the hidden figure or animal. Deek's double image cards work this way: when the card is sloped to the left dogs appear, when sloped to the right cats appear or the moon changes its facial expression. There are actual jig-saw puzzles made up of thirty to forty separate pieces, X-ray illusion cards, invisible pictures brought out either by heat ('magic') or by rubbing with a coin ('frictographs'), and cards that actually set problems or puzzles.

6. A stereoscopic viewer so popular in late Victorian times was used to look at the twin view stereoscopic postcards with similar pictures. A variation consisted of red and green images superimposed which could be viewed through red and green gelatine eye-pieces. A green Australian bush cascade is seen through the red eye piece and a red dusky beauty appears in the green one. Then there are cards with mirror writing, one of a rather

unhappy little boy which when held to the mirror says, 'Never got that letter you didn't write me!'

Numerous models can be found on postcards, some to cut out and some with partial perforations which allow the butterflies or birds to be pushed upright. There are bathing beauties with two holes for fingers to be pushed through to form realistic legs, or Charlie's Aunt where the end of the finger produces a very bulbous nose. Even the embossed card is basically a novelty. The amplified version of it known as the bas-relief is certainly so, especially when the portrait is decorated with brightly-coloured jewels or tinsel.

The pull-out card is always popular, especially where the little concertina pack of views inside deals with a specialised subject, such as hop-picking or the Boy Scout code. Many of these pull-outs are cut to the shape of an animal, bathing machine, a trunk or lighthouse. There are in fact all sorts of shapes and sizes in postcards, the sizes ranging from the square midget types and oblong book-marks, through the folding panoramic cards to the giants, measuring nearly twelve inches by nine inches—but were still able to travel to their destination for one halfpenny. The most popular of these

*Windsor Castle from appliquéd bus tickets, London Service 35 visible on right; the conductor punched a hole against your destination, say Lombard St. (in middle of Round Tower).*

*A finely embossed Washington commemorative, Tuck's George Washington's Birthday' No. 124. Even embossing was a form of novelty to sell more cards.*

*A delightful hand-painted greeting on celluloid, the trees thickly stippled with white for added effect.*

*A bas-relief, the dress hand-coloured, and appliquéd with powdered crystal or diamanté, which glints and gleams.*

*A printed satin shield appliquéd within a lovely Art Nouveau frame, Tuck series 8854.*

39

giant cards are the Rotary and Philco series of colour photographic actresses.

Quite a collection of silhouettes can be assembled and many portrait studies were cut on the spot in large stores, such as D. H. Evans in Oxford Street, London, by artists like Handrup or Le Baron Henri Scotford. Finally, there were perfumed sachets, cards with holes for the insertion of photographs or to which a photograph could be glued, and a number of special patent types such as the Valentine 'Kissogram'.

## SILK AND SATIN CARDS

The silk postcard was also designed as a novelty and these fall into separate categories according to the type of manufacture, ie. woven, embroidered or printed.

The most expensive card is the woven postcard and two English firms in particular, E. Stevens and W. H. Grant produced a most varied selection including views, personalities, exhibitions and ships. The earliest continental silks date from 1898 and those with Art Nouveau designs are most sought and expensive. The French exploited the field more than anyone else but there are also Japanese silks and some for the St. Louis 1904 World Fair in the United States.

There are far more embroidered silk cards than woven ones but they are usually later in date although the first one was patented in Switzerland in 1900 by Buff and Mitler of Zurich. There are thousands of different greetings and patriotic cards, and most regiments are represented in the military series. More is paid for designs that are specific with ships, zeppelins, Santa Claus and what are termed the flame types, representing churches and cathedrals being burned in France during the First World War. This was the time when the embroidered silk was sent through the post in transparent envelopes by thousands of service men on the continent to their families and loved ones at home. Some enhanced the novelty aspect by inserting in the envelope type of embroidered silk a small card with an artistic design on it which could be used for a short message. Others included a silk handkerchief.

The least collected type of silk card is the printed one. Those of film stars and of Edith Cavell, the nurse who was killed during the First World War, are not especially attractive. But there are some better cards, especially those where the silk is an oval view of a glamorous girl or is in the shape of a shield set within a gilded or art nouveau frame.

A special type of printed satin card was manufactured for Sharpes of Bradford and called the FAB Patchwork card. Any number of these patches could be stitched together to make tablecloths, cushion covers and bedspreads and just one could be used as a form of decoration on pockets, pincushions or teacosies. The ones most sought are the heraldic arms of towns and clan badges in Series A and personalities in Series P., and after these the extensive range of flowers in Series F and views in Series V.

A quite separate series of Spanish cards are embroidered directly on to the top layer of the postcard utilising hundreds of minute holes forming the design, which is usually the dress of a Spanish beauty. The modern equivalents are still being sold in Spain today.

# 9   Entertainment and Leisure

About the only picture you will not find on the early postcard is the
television screen, but every other form of entertainment is there in plenty,
whether indoor or outdoor. Since, like every other subject, the collecting
field is immense, it is wise to consider it under various subdivisions.

## THEATRE, MUSIC HALL AND GROUPS

When the postcard became popular, the theatre was at its height, and its
stars everyday household names. There would be no difficulty in collecting
a thousand cards each for most of the following actors and actresses:

| | |
|---|---|
| Arundale, Sybil | Jeffries, Maud |
| Ashwell, Lena | Langtry, Lily |
| Aylwin, Jean | Lessing, Madge |
| Brayton, Lily | Love, Mabel |
| Burke, Billie | Mason, Delia |
| Chase, Pauline | May, Edna |
| Collier, Constance | Millar, Gertie |
| Cooper, Gladys | Millard, Evelyn |
| Crichton, Madge | Neilson, Julia |
| Dare, Phyllis | Oliver, Ethel |
| Dare, Zena | Ray, Gabrielle |
| Elliott, Gertrude | Rowlands, Gaynor |
| Elsie, Lily | Sevening, Nina |
| Gordon, Kitty | Studholme, Marie |
| Green, Mabel | Tempest, Marie |
| Harvey, Martin | Terriss, Ellaline |
| Hicks, Seymour | Vanburgh, Irene |
| Jay, Isabel | Waller, Lewis |

On the other hand, there are many personalities quite difficult to locate on
picture postcards for one reason or another, and there are some not so
difficult to find but still in great demand today for which you may well have
to pay ten times the price of any on the above list. In the former category is
the comedian Herbert Campbell, who died in 1904 and in the latter group
Marie Lloyd, the famous music hall star, and the French actress Sarah
Bernhardt. Also very popular, but not so expensive, are Dan Leno, George
Robey and Henry Irving.

Because there are so many theatrical postcards you may wish to make a
selection of the best series available. There are thousands of real
photograph cards and it is simply a matter of choosing those where the
expression or dress of your favourite actress is to your liking. There is a
smaller number of colour cards and some of them are very poorly produced,
but the Misch series 'Famous Beauties' is worthwhile and Taylor's
Orthochrome has many fine chromo-litho portraits. The Tuck series

41

'Celebrities of the Stage' appeared in various formats but the colour glosso and photochrome series are two of the best types. Beagles' produced cards in colour with a gilded background and Bamforth's issued a colour series where the dresses have gilded decorations. Hildesheimer (pronounced Hildes-hymer) had an attractive colour series and there are quite a number of photograph cards where the dresses have been pleasantly tinted. Again, it is a matter of choosing those types where the work has been well done, for this can make such a difference to the final result. A range of actress cards which are quite worth while, though often French in origin, have the portrait set in attractive frames, frequently with art nouveau elements. For early portraits the very long Rotary series of matt photographs on undivided backs is to be recommended.

Sometimes the story behind a particular card is worth rediscovering. An example of this is a picture of Miss May Yohe on a Rapid Photo Company postcard. Miss Yohe was Lady Frances Hope, who wore the world famous Hope Diamond. Her conduct earned her a notorious name, and she later married Captain Putman Bradley Strong of the U.S. Army. She ended up in Sacramento, California, doing a cheap song and dance turn in the local vaudeville theatre. What a change from her days of fame!

The messages on theatrical cards are often worth checking. Besides finding some from famous personalities themselves, they often give tit-bits of information about theatrical life which can be interesting or amusing. One card posted from the London Hippodrome in October 1913 says, 'Everything is going splendidly, except that one of our girls fell into the orchestra last week!' On a postcard depicting Gaynor Rowlands, postmarked 4th August 1906, the message reads, "This actress died the week before last through an operation." A photographic card published by Guy and Company of Cork, Eire, shows Lily Elsie on horseback. After pointing this out, the writer continues, "She and her husband, Ian Bullough, rent a house in the hunting season near here called 'Oakgrove'".

As well as portrait cards there are sets for almost every play and show that was staged, and there are fine colour poster advertisements to put at the head of each such collection. Especially sought are cards for the Gilbert and Sullivan Light Operas, some of which are multi-views, featuring several characters on each card. Multi-views are sometimes more desirable than single ones, particularly where, as in the case of Nesta Verney 'The Dapper Little Male Impersonator' you can see her as a woman flanked by two examples in her male role. The montage style was also frequently used for commemoratives and In Memoriam cards.

A collection of theatres can be linked with the plays staged there, especially where playbills are readable. A picture of the Moulin Rouge in Paris proclaims in large letters 'La-Belle-de-New-York'. French cards of actresses and dancing girls often give the name of the theatre with which they were usually associated, such as 'Les Ambassadeurs', 'Folies Bergere', and 'Marigny'. Many provincial theatres are less easy to find but they are good prizes if the building no longer exists.

A type of card which fits into this context, is that of the strolling player, and varied groups that formed in the provinces and during the summer at most seaside towns. They range from 'The Highwaymen', 'The Yokels', 'The

*The Theatre Royal, Haymarket, London, with (l to r) Carrie Moore, Gertie Millar, Edna May, Marie Studholme, Zena Dare and Phyllis Dare all added to the foreground of the photo.*

*Exotic Anna Held, who from Music Hall rose to stardom with Ziegfeld in Broadway's smash hit 'A Parlor Match', featuring 'The Man Who Broke the Bank at Monte Carlo'.*

*A typical Edwardian colonial picnic; note the gay biscuit tins and small accordion.*

*The Bronco Buster–being given a hard time of it.*

Sparks', through 'Les Vivandiers', 'The Yorkshire Pierrots', to 'Rushberry's Uncle Toms Cabin Company' and the 'Royal Rumanian Band'. You can tie in actual seaside performances to often very large crowds, and thus follow the famous White Coons from Clacton-on-Sea to Bray, County Wicklow.

Individual performances are even more varied. There is Jimmy Dyer, the Cumberland Bard playing his violin at your front door, or Private George Doughty R.M.L.I. playing the piano non-stop for twelve hours in July 1913. There are midgets and giants a-plenty, Miss Etta in her famous disrobing act on the trapeze or Mr. Sloper the Ventriloquist with his seven dolls. The magician Claude Delvin, demonstrates his cup and ball tricks and so does Mlle. Hencleur's Company of twelve dogs.

## CINEMA AND CIRCUS

The picture postcard was in decline when the cinema became popular, so although there is a full range depicting the early cinema stars, they are not found in such quantity as actors and actresses and so they cost considerably more. Charlie Chaplin and Shirley Temple must rank as the most popular but Laurel and Hardy, Rudolph Valentino and Ramon Navarro come close behind. Early cinemas are also more expensive than theatres, often because they were converted buildings which lacked the permanency of the average theatre and by the time the later more definitive cinemas appeared, most postcard publishers were no longer interested in them. The best view of an early cinema will include some of the posters advertising the early films.

The Walt Disney films are represented by some fine colour postcards and

43

although these only date from the 1930s onwards, they are very collectable and fetch good prices, particularly Snow White and the Seven Dwarfs. There is also a good series of Felix the Cat.

There are a number of circus cards showing clowns and various acts and there are advertising cards for the Royal Italian Circus, Buffalo Bill's Wild West Show, and best of all the Barnum and Bailey posters, many of which are multi-view in the Gruss aus style.

## MUSIC AND LITERARY SUBJECTS

Music is well represented on picture postcards with a wide range of classical composers, famous musicians and orchestras, and many scenes from operas and ballets. You will have no difficulty in finding postcards of Clara Butt or Jan Kubelik, but it is much harder to locate Enrico Caruso or Sir Henry Wood, despite the fact that they may receive the same valuation in postcard catalogues.

Song cards were often issued in sets of three or four, recording the verses of each song along with a picture to illustrate the main theme. Bamforth issued hundreds of colour sets of three or four cards each, along with some pairs and singles, and other publishers issued photographic types. Some cards show the music as well, and others just give the title of the song with a picture to illustrate its theme.

There are plenty of bands of all types—military, dance and jazz. Bandstands themselves make an interesting theme around which to build a collection, because many of them no longer exist today, and those that do are continually under a threat of destruction as costs of preservation go on rising. The early gramophone is another very popular theme and finding genuine indoor scenes with a gramophone in the picture is very difficult.

Literary subjects are also best classified under Leisure, and if you choose William Shakespeare or Charles Dickens, you need to budget for up to one thousand cards, for anything like completion. You can also build a sizeable collection for Sir Walter Scott, Robert Burns, Alfred Tennyson, Thomas Hardy, Mark Twain or R. D. Blackmore's Lorna Doone. For each of these authors, there are many character studies, and background scenes of plays and the books themselves. Raphael Tuck published sets entitled, 'In Shakespeare's Country' and 'In Dickens' Land'.

There are a number of general series too. Tuck published an early chromo-lithograph series, 'Famous Writers and Poets', and a later one, 'Homes of Literary Men'. Blum and Dagen issued an 'Eminent Writers' series.

Alice in Wonderland is a natural subject for the picture postcard and every angle seems to have been exploited. This is the sort of theme that can overflow into a rich variety of other subjects including advertising and politics. If the last heading sounds surprising, then what about 'The Kaiser's Adventures in Wonderland', (with apologies to Lewis Carroll), a set of twelve designed by Violette Cotton consisting of cartoons based on the characters in the book. There is an argument when Alice appears carrying the cake marked 'Belgium'; the Kaiser stands on his head to the famous Old Father William rhyme, and Alice acts as mediator between Tweedledum and Tweedledee, who are fighting over Great Britain's rattle. Some of the most famous lines are slightly altered thus: "What matters it how far we

44

go", his winged friend replied, "There is another shore you know upon the other side. The further off from England, the nearer is to France. Will you, Won't you, Will you, Won't you, Won't you join the dance?"

## SPORTS AND PASTIMES

The picture postcard catches every aspect of sport imaginable, including many of the stars of yesteryear. There are individual portraits and action shots of famous cricketers, footballers, golfers, tennis stars, athletes, boxers, wrestlers and other less well-known games. Ink autographed cards are most sought, and naturally cost more.

You can collect famous race-horses, become an expert in the art of bull-fighting, walk from London to Brighton, or Land's End to John O'Groats, climb every mountain, enjoy the Henley Regatta, or the Oxford University Eight-Oar bumping races. Perhaps you would prefer to share in the sports at Crystal Palace, carrying twelve fruit baskets on your head without dropping them (illustrated), or be a spectator at any one of the Olympic Games from 1896 onwards. You can trace through the history of the bicycle or assemble a collection of all types of yachts and pleasure craft, or follow

*Golf cards are eagerly sought; Harry Vardon (lower right) won 'The Open' six times between 1896 and 1914.*

*The Fruit Basket Race at Crystal Palace, which could also be seen every day at Covent Garden Market, though not for fun there.*

*A Brussels-style pillar box of the 1850s; the address on the letter is that of W. S. Lincoln, who issued some of the earliest stamp catalogues.*

*The playing card theme is always popular.*

*Reproducing Britain's stamps on postcards published in this country was forbidden; this is a rare case that may have escaped because all the stamps were used ones (Hill of Sunderland).*

45

horse and hound with many named Hunts featuring a large number of personalised real photographs.

When it comes to indoor games, there is just as much variety. Billiards and snooker, ping-pong or table tennis, gymnastics, draughts and crossword puzzles, roller-skating and ice-skating. Two most popular themes seem to be playing cards and chess, the last subject being particularly difficult to locate, and then it is often found that the chess masters are cats and dogs.

The collecting theme itself is well covered on postcards. Bank notes and coins of most nations of the world can be found with many embossed, silvered and gilded. The stamp collector also has several series of colourful embossed stamp cards, and the best of these contain a view or map surrounded by the stamps of that country, often depicting a complete set. Even Cinderella stamps appear on picture postcards, as for example, the Paris exposition labels of 1900. A fine collection can be made of actual Cinderella stamps, in many cases affixed to the picture side. There were also special issues of stamp postcards for many of the philatelic exhibitions in various countries. Another branch of this subject is 'The Language of Stamps', displaying the varied romantic messages that could be conveyed, according to the angle at which one placed the stamp.

*John Ruskin, author and artist (died 1900), an Abraham photo.*

*W. Day with original Lumiere Projector used for first regular show of moving pictures in Britain 20th Feb. 1896–autographed by him.*

*The key figure of the early postcard world in Britain at his desk–autographed by E. W. Richardson, editor* **The Picture Postcard.**

*Watch Tower, Beachy Head, Eastbourne, once used for signalling. A Picture Post Card stall when this was taken.*

*A French Postcard Shop–photo by Louis Levy, a much collected publisher.*

A letter from the famous house of Tuck about an error on a postcard, which they hoped to correct in a third edition. It is addressed to W. Reginald Bray, of Forest Hill, London, who was collecting postcards by at least 1898, most of which were used to obtain autographs from people in the picture or connected with the buildings shown. Called The Autograph King, he claimed the largest collection of modern autographs in the world, and exhibited at many exhibitions. Each card was consecutively numbered, and by April 1924 he had amassed 16,289 autographs, mostly on postcards. Notice the many reviews quoted down the right-hand side of the letter, which continue right down the back too, 24 in all, mostly over just a two-month period.

The cartologist will undoubtedly consider that postcard collecting makes the most interesting theme. He can collect publishers' blanks and samples, postcards on postcards, postcard shops, cards issued by machines, postcards advertising publishers, incorrect captions and spelling, errors and alterations, actual artist originals as well as proof editions which Tuck made a special feature of, postcard competitions, and modern postcard dealers' specimens. Most sought after of all are the early cards commemorating postcard exhibitions.

An interesting series of matched pairs can be collected. A publishers' proof with a plain back and often without any caption can often be matched with the issued card. Picture alterations can form a subject in themselves where exactly the same picture has had certain features removed and others added. Perhaps a horse tram has been replaced by an electric tram, or people in the picture have been added or deleted. Sometimes only half a person has been removed, leaving just the head and shoulders, or a pair of legs! Even trebles can be collected, showing a scene in daylight, the same with snow added, and a third type where darkness descends, the lights are lit and the moon comes out. This way the publisher obtained three selling lines for the price of one basic photograph.

## FESTIVALS AND GREETINGS

There are greetings cards for every occasion and they come in a wide variety. Some plain and others lightly embossed, some deeply embossed and additionally gilded and silvered to make a card of superb quality. Besides the usual festivals and anniversaries, there are a number of special ones such as:

| | |
|---|---|
| April Fool's Day | Jewish New Year |
| Decoration Day | Leap Year |
| Empire Day | St. Patrick's Day |
| Halloween | Thanksgiving Day |
| Independence Day (4th July) | Valentine's Day |

Some of the most keenly sought cards are those depicting Santa Claus engaged in his various activities, usually dressed in his red cloak, but quite often in other colours too.

A number of special greetings types are worth the collectors' consideration. Some carry a colourful embossed border of shells or fish, which surrounds a central picture of a town or seaside resort. In America a similar border is formed by an alligator and this series is particularly popular. Many designs are made up of tree or plant leaves or butterflies, and in the centre of each one is a small view; these are often printed by chromolithography.

The 'Hands across the Sea' type is another popular greeting form intended to bring together the peoples and nations separated by the oceans. They can be linked with any collection that stresses communication for they often depict ships and trains, the continents and even the globe itself.

This is where the new collector of picture postcards comes to appreciate that he will not find his subject neatly delineated for him under one heading in a dealer's box or album. Imagination is needed in order to exploit to the full every theme that a collector has decided to pursue.

# 10    Government, Ceremony and Armed Forces

Very few kings exist today in countries throughout the world. In the heyday of the picture postcard there were many more and the Royalty cult had a very considerable following. Plenty of portraits exist of all the members of royal families, down to the very least significant, and there is a greater proportion of real photographic types, matt or glossy. There are numerous family groups, and children can be followed through from their early years into adulthood. The best pictures are the dated occasions where all the individuals are named.

Of the many cards showing royal visits, the most valuable are those taken by small local publishers on private occasions. All special visits to towns and cities are of interest to collectors of local events. Occasions for national ceremonial, such as coronations and funerals, are the least popular types and are frequently over-valued in postcard catalogues.

The most important royalty cards are the commemorative issues, usually in colour, often embossed and exhibiting a pleasing design. The problem for the beginner is to distinguish the common ones from the scarce and even rare, so it is as well to study what is offered by a number of dealers before starting to collect them. An example of a rare Edward VII Coronation commemorative is *illustrated*. Due to the change in date of the coronation, this card was never actually issued, as the message states.

One of the most outstanding series of royalty cards is the 'Kings and Queens of England', issued by Tuck. Superbly printed by chromolithography, it illustrates thirty-seven of the principal Kings and Queens up to and including Edward VII, and was issued as a coronation souvenir in 1902. Another long series was issued by the King Insurance Company and consists of fifty cards, again ending with King Edward VII. This is a most imaginative set with illuminations drawn from ancient manuscripts, the Bayeaux Tapestry, paintings, coins, engravings, relics, tombs and even a stained glass window.

The best Royalty advertising cards were all issued in connection with King Edward VII's Coronation, and include a set of six Lemco Coronation Souvenirs, four fine vignettes issued by Birds' Custard, and eight cards published by Weldons' Bazaar.

Many foreign royalty cards are rated more highly than English ones and this especially applies to Russian and East European countries and some of the smaller countries like Siam. There is a considerable number of German royalty cards for each of the states and royal houses. Spain, Portugal and the Low Countries are well down in popularity.

## POLITICS
Although it is so closely related the political scene seems to have produced a different kind of card. There are the portraits of leading figures as usual

49

*A rare Edward VII Coronation card, prepared by Vollenweider of Algeria, but never published due to the change in date.*

*Gladstone helped to make the postcard acceptable; some collectors like 'error' cards–the date of birth here should be Dec. 29th 1809.*

*One of the most difficult 'Royal' personalities to find on postcard.*

*Unlike most election cards, this one even adds the results.*

*Mafeking Siege banknotes and stamps, mementos of the Boer War.*

and some particularly fine sets of the Presidents of the United States. There are also a number of cards used in elections, showing the candidates and their claims, and even a few that give the results of an election, as on the card *illustrated* from Boston, Lincolnshire.

The principal interest however, centres around the various political campaigns for and against reforms of one kind or another. Highest of all come the Suffragette cards, with portraits of the leaders, demonstrations in Hyde Park and Trafalgar Square and scenes of their arrest. Then there is a wide variety of comic and cartoon cards. Another issue at that time which sadly still claims so much attention, was Home Rule for Ireland. There are scenes of the Irish uprising and pictures of destruction and ruin. John Bull frequently features in cartoons connected with the Free Trade and Protection issues, which so often dominated British politics in the first decade of this century.

The world-wide political scene is well represented on postcards, with cartoons, commemorative cards and actual scenes of events. There are Boer War cartoons, the famous Dreyfus Trial in France, The Boxer Rising in China in 1900, the seventy-fifth anniversary of Belgian independence in

1905, and in the same year the St. Petersburg Revolt in Russia and the Referendum to separate Norway from Sweden. The First World War produced many cartoons and patriotic cards from the Rape of Belgium through to the Victory Celebrations.

Cards for later events are more difficult to find, as for example, those connected with the Spanish Civil War. One interesting colour card, published in 1938, shows a Catalonian couple joining with John Bull and Uncle Sam in the Union of Democratic Nations, expressing the hope that it would end war for ever *(illustrated)*. We are only too well aware of the failure of that hope. An American card posted in Detroit in 1940 urges the recipient to vote for Harold E. Stoll and a montage of illustrations depict his re-organisation of the Register of Deeds Office.

Many cards commemorate Empire Day in Britain and Independence Day in America and there are In Memoriam cards for prominent politicians, like President William McKinley, who was assassinated in 1901, and special souvenir cards like that for W. E. Gladstone *(illustrated)*. Early cards of Winston Churchill are not easy to find and particularly when they also show Miss Clementine Hozier, the girl he married *(illustrated)*.

The Chinese Boxer Rebellion of 1900.

*A cartoon about the famous Dreyfus case that rocked France in the 1890s.*

*Early views of Churchill can be quite expensive, especially with the girl he was to marry.*

*The Spanish Civil War, John Bull and Uncle Sam join in hoping 1938 will bring peace to Spain.*

## HERALDRY AND FLAGS

Even if you just collect cards of your own locality, you will want to include a few which show the Coats-of-Arms of your own and neighbouring towns. Several different series exist, one of the best and most comprehensive being the Ja-Ja Series. Those that are termed 'Full-Out' pictures carry nothing else except the full colour Coat-of-Arms, but other cards reduce the crest and add a view of the town or city alongside. Tuck issued a very fine embossed chromo series covering the principal towns and cities of the British Isles, with a sepia view added to many of them; there are also cards for America and France. There is a fine French colour series, called 'Collection Heraldique', and an excellent German series has a colour embossed and gilded arms in one corner and a chromo-litho view, set within a wide border. Most countries have multi-arms cards depicting all the Swiss Cantons badges, or the arms of the Netherlands provinces and principal towns, or the crests of Oxford or Cambridge University Colleges.

Two sets of pottery models also feature many towns and cities. The Trent models are set against green or brown backgrounds, the best ones having a partially gilded frame. Better still are the Goss pottery cards with numbers one to six, not too difficult to obtain; numbers seven and eight are very scarce indeed and worth double the value of the others. An interesting sideline to this collection is to locate street scenes with shops that sold Goss China. Usually there is a tin badge displayed outside as in the case of the shop in Market Place, Ilminster, or a larger sign with 'Goss China' in large white letters, for example, Addisons in Chertsey Road, Woking.

There are hundreds of miscellaneous crests ranging from the ducal arms for the House of Lords issued by Tuck, to that of the Order of the Knights of the Round Table of King Arthur, or the West Indies cricket team. A series of thirty cards displays the standards of the members of the Order of the Garter.

Flags of all nations can be collected in several series, probably the largest is that published by the Aristophot Company, with more than four hundred different designs. The best sets are printed by chromo-lithography and a series by Guggenheim and Company of Zurich is embossed with a small sepia view let into one corner. Another French series uses the entire card surface for the flag, adds in the centre the coat-of-arms, and in a small circular inset depicts the national costume. One of the finest series of 'Arms

*An unusual heraldic card, published by Porritt Brothers in Yorkshire.*

*Even Prisoner of War camps had their emblems; this card was advertising the post card publisher's life story.*

*Alderney (Channel Isles) cards are hard to find, especially with good postmarks.*

52

of the Nations' was publishedby Paul Kohl; Tuck re-issued a number of these with English captions.

There are many sets of 'State Girls', covering each one of the United States, along with the shield and coat-of-arms. The best of these was published by the Langsdorf Company. A set of Tuck College Kings and Queens depicts them as playing cards.

This is perhaps the best place to mention the excellent range of tartan cards for Scotland. Again, Tuck excel with a series with inset views, but Johnston of Edinburgh published two interesting series, one illustrating the arms, tartan and badge of each clan along with a representative clansman or clanswoman, and a later series with an overall tartan background, an inset map showing the territory of the clan, with arms on the other side—a very effective combination. Vignettes of colourful clansmen in action appear on the McIan's Highland series, which is rather difficult to find.

## MILITARY

You can collect more than a thousand military cards issued by one specialist publisher alone, Gale and Polden of Aldershot. If you wanted to collect cards of World War I, you could probably amass at least ten thousand. Not only could you bring together picture postcards showing every war since the Boer War, but you could find pictures of most historic battles, painted by a wide variety of artists.

Indeed, the colour artist cards are the most popular of all military types.

*The Boer War battle for Ladysmith; note the photographer fleeing at lower-right.*

*A superb chromo map linked with the Boer War, very much sought by collectors.*

*Gale & Polden's 'British Army' series, often called 'History and Traditions'; the Yeomanry cards are some of the most difficult to find.*

*Another difficult Gale & Polden series—medals and orders.*

Sets have been issued covering most regiments and an outstanding series published by Gale and Polden gives the history and traditions of each one. Another long series by the same firm shows the badges of each regiment and a shorter matching set, less easy to obtain, depicts the principal medals and orders that could be won. Another long series of badges, with a brief history of the regiment beneath each one, was published during the First World War by the British Photogram Company of Exeter; these are difficult to find.

Exploits in winning the Victoria Cross form the subject of several series, and a historical set tracing types of 'The King's Army', at various dates and published by Valentine is alive with action scenes, The Light Brigade at Balaclava or Cavaliers at Naseby. These cards were drawn by J. A. Stewart, one of a number of specialist military artists and a list of some of the best of these from many countries follows:

| | | | |
|---|---|---|---|
| Baertsoen, A. | C | Luschwitz-Koreffski, A. | B |
| Baker, Granville H. | B | McNeill, J. | B |
| Barty | C | Meissonier, J. L. E. | B |
| Bastien, A. T. | C | Munnings, A. J. | B |
| Becker, C. | A | Neumann, Fritz | B |
| Chambry, Paul | B | O'Beirne, F. | A |
| Chidley, A. | B | Palma de Rosa, A. | B |
| Dupuis, Emil | A | Paulus, P. | C |
| Fouqueray, Charles | B | Pàyne, Harry | A |
| Fourquiers, J. | A | Piffàrd, H. | B |
| Foussaint, Maurice | C | Ralston, William | A |
| Geens, Louis | B | Rowlandson, G. D. | B |
| Hardy, F. C. | B | Simkin, R. | A |
| Henckel, Carl | A | Stewart, J. A. | B |
| Holloway, Edgar H. | B | Stuckelberger, W. | A |
| Howard, C. T. | C | Thirlar, James | B |
| Hudson, Gerald | B | Toussaint, M. | A |
| Ibbetson, Ernest | A | Vallet, Louis | A |
| Leigh, Conrad | C | Wagemans, M. | C |
| Leroux, Pierre A. | C | Ward, Herbert | C |
| Lloyd, T. Ivester | C | Wollen, W. B. | B |
| Love, H. Montagu | B | Wood, Stanley, L. | B |
| Lovett, A. C. | C | Woodville, R. Caton | B |
| Lumley, S. | B | | |

The cards of World War I cover every possible theme imaginable. Because of censorship many of the newspapers issued popular series of official pictures. Of these, the Daily Mail series is the longest and is best collected in colour where available, rather than the more common sepia edition A set by Newspaper Illustrations consists of forty-eight cards in sepia and twenty-four in colour. One of the finest series was published by the Photochrom Company and entitled 'On Active Service'. It is easily distinguished by the yellow border. Another series of Naval postcards of the British Fleet in the North Sea, were reproduced from the film entitled 'Britain Prepared'.

Hundreds of cards were issued to help in raising funds for many

*A fine military poster with nicely balanced design.*

*An earlier naval battle round the Falkland Islands–in December 1914, when four German cruisers were sunk (seen centre).*

organisations connected with the war effort, and all the various campaigns in France, Salonika, the Dardanelles, Palestine and Mesopotamia are represented. There are groups of cards showing war damage on the continent and a few for Great Britain, the result of Zeppelin raids in the South and East. A list of types can be extended indefinitely with prominent personalities, prisoner-of-war camps, special greetings, patriotic and sentimental cards and even recruiting posters.

An interesting sideline is to trace through the many temporary camps that existed in Britain, as numerous local cards were issued, showing activities both serious and humorous. For collectors specialising in a local area this is an aspect frequently forgotten, but very rewarding because the cards are often cheap and published only in limited editions.

By comparison, there are very few cards for the Second World War, but once again a notable series was issued by Photochrom entitled 'London Under Fire'. These illustrated some of the worst areas devasted by bombing, including the immediate area around the once famous home of Tuck—Raphael House, which with all its records, was destroyed on the 29th December 1940.

A whole range of cards cover scenes of life with the humorous and hilarious well catered for. For many years a series of cards traced each of the Aldershot Tattoos and the Royal Tournament, as well as other tattoos like Tidworth.

For overseas military cards the number and variety of Italian Regimentals is hard to beat. There is a rich variety of cards covering the Russo-Japanese War of 1904–1905. There are some fine early French series printed by chromo-lithography.

## NAVY AND AIR FORCE

The world's navies are naturally well represented on postcard and here the real photograph once again triumphs. The British, United States, German and French Fleets predominate but ships of other nations can be collected.

Great sea actions of World War I form a prominent part of Naval History on postcards. The one *illustrating* the Falkland Islands' Battle is a fine multi-view issued by one of the best publishers of naval postcards, Abrahams of Devonport. A similar one shows the events of the naval raid on Zeebrugge on the 23rd April 1918. The scuttling of the German fleet at Scapa Flow in June 1919 is well depicted on a photographic series by C. W. Burrows.

Naval history would not be complete if the famous exploits of Nelson were omitted. There are hundreds of cards on this one theme alone and for the Nelson Centenary in 1905 some very fine ones were issued, including Tuck Oilettes. An early series of chromo-litho vignettes is easily distinguished by a gilded border. The principal events of his life are recounted, including his leaving home to go to sea for the first time in 1771.

The Air Force did not have the prominence during World War I that it obtained between 1939 and 1945, so the usual situation is reversed and there are many more cards for aircraft of the second war. Earlier cards relate to the Royal Flying Corps, and were inclined to poke a little fun at this new institution which had yet to prove itself. This is reflected on a series issued by Birn Brothers with black and white sketches and embossed gilded badges.

The Military Airship was much in use before the First World War and there are some fine photographic cards of these issued by two Aldershot firms, William May and Gale & Polden. The Zeppelins should not be forgotten, and many cards with special stamps, postmarks and cachets are also of interest to the philatelist.

It can safely be said that no single aspect of the First World War at home or abroad is missing from the annals of the picture postcard. Rationing, mascots, the part played by the women, pin-ups, the songs, even a set of maps issued by The Bystander, showing the advances and reverses of the opposing armies, with the arrows neatly personified as the French and German leaders *(illustrated)*. Perhaps the best footnote to this whole sad episode of human history is that showing the German navy taking root, with rusting battleships and grass growing through the decks. An ancient, bearded sailor asks another octogenarian, "Say, Fritz, Ven are ve going to cut the grass again?"

# 11 Transport and Exploration

It is fortunate for the picture postcard that its Golden Age coincided with remarkable advances by mankind in various fields. The history of aviation can almost be told from its first page through postcards. The early grotesque flying machines are seen in flight but more often on the ground. The first aviation meetings in Britain and France are well recorded as well as the tours sponsored by the Daily Mail in 1912 and 1913. Hendon in North-West London was then a prominent centre for early aviators, and there is a fine photographic series 'Flying at Hendon'.

The airship too is well documented, and especially the numerous French experiments. Some of the tragic early accidents were also captured by the photographer. For example, a double width panoramic postcard depicts the collapse of Santos Dumont's airship over the south coast of France in 1902. Many messages on postcards preserve the testimony of early eye-witnesses. A card posted from Sydenham, London on the 10th September 1910 states, "Just as I arrived at Penge, Moisson, The American, with his aeroplane, arrived at Crystal Palace, in the distance he looked like a large crow. He flew most gracefully, whilst circling round, he passed over the garden".

With the interest in first flights, special cachets and postmarks collected by philatelists, a very comprehensive collection can be put together. It has to be remembered that most aviation postcards are expensive, so that it might be wiser to select a more limited theme, such as the history of the flying boat, or the Schneider Trophy Races, which were staged over many years, (excluding World War I), and from a speed of 44 miles per hour attained in 1913, a figure of 328 miles per hour was achieved in 1929.

## ROAD TRANSPORT

You can start here with the Stone Age if you like, in a series 'The Evolution of the Motor-Car', drawn by G. E. Studdy, in 1902. Or you may prefer to begin with the great age of coaching, a complete enough subject in itself. Many artists' cards depict the stage coach, staging posts and old coaching inns, particularly a set of sixteen drawn by the renowned John Charles Maggs (1819-1896). Tuck also issued a series of 'Picturesque Coaching Inns'. You can include a coach meet in London's Hyde Park, the grave at Boxmoor, Hertfordshire, of the last Highwayman, Robert Snooks, and the memorial statue in the River Wyley, near Salisbury, where a stage coach overturned and the driver was drowned.

Many excellent photographic postcards show the last of the stage coaches like the Lynton and Minehead, the Ilfracombe to Lynton (North Devon) or the Roughton to Cromer in Norfolk. Attempts to revive the stage coach include Vanderbilt's Coach 'Venture' from Brighton to London in 1908 and the Reliance from Guildford to London. The change from stage coach to horse bus is reflected mainly in the type of vehicle used and the lack of uniform, horn and flourish. Thus the 'Express', running from Partridge Green to Brighton, every Tuesday and Friday, looks more like a glorified cart although it was drawn by two fine horses.

Close-up photographic pictures of early horse-buses are well worth collecting when you can find them, but don't despise the private carts and carriages which make a fine theme in themselves. There are gigs and phaetons, landaus and broughams, dog carts and buggies and most distinctive of all, the famous Hansom cab, the 'Taxi' of the horse age.

There exists a great variety of hand carts used by tradesmen and the interesting shapes of those used by the postman, the milkman and the baker certainly remind one of a forgotten era. Along with close-ups, you can find many street scenes featuring these carts.

The bicycle must not be forgotten. Here too, there were many unusual shapes and a postcard showing a penny-farthing bicycle is indeed a prize. There were several different types of bicycle and a special model used for postmen, and there are later postcards showing the tandem. Cycle racing was more popular then than it is today, except in France.

Before the motor-car, steam traction had its day, and a fine close-up of an early traction engine like the one *illustrated* is very scarce. You can however, often find an inexpensive street scene, perhaps of London, which includes a steam lorry or a steam bus.

The early car is not as popular a subject as one would expect. Certainly it was very well photographed, and it seems that one of the first things that a proud new owner did was to commission a photograph, which was printed as a picture postcard. Frequently, a photograph was taken when a happy group of holiday-makers took a ride in a local motor charabanc. The value of these cards is greatly enhanced when the make of the vehicle is clearly evident and more so still if the registration number can be read.

The early motor races are well represented, especially those in France—the Peking to Paris race and the Gordon Bennett races. Not so easy to find are maps of the race courses like the one *illustrated,* or the special commemorative cards issued, such as The International Tourist Trophy Race run on the 30th May 1907, which *illustrates* the winning car, number 22, a 20 horse power Rover. The Photochrom Company issued several series of colour cards of notable racing cars.

Because of the popularity of tram postcards, good ones have rocketed in value over the last few years, but the tram or trolley-car enthusiast is usually only interested in close-up pictures or foreground views clearly showing the number of the tram. Many local collectors naturally include trams in street scenes but if you want to make a small tram collection, it would be wiser to collect just the smaller systems which operated a mere handful of vehicles. Although these are difficult to find, the average dealer doesn't charge any extra, for he seldom realizes the difference.

There are not so many buses on postcard, for by the time the bus took over from the electric tram the postcard was in decline. Many companies promoted their services by issuing advertising postcards, which usually included a picture of a sample vehicle. The trolley bus or railless trolley is also hard to find, especially early examples.

The Golden Age of Postcards saw many
notable changes through new inventions,
especially in modes of transport.

A pricey category–a steam traction wagon
belonging to Twyford Mills, from the
Chester area.

Route for one of the early French motor
races in the Gordon-Bennett trials.

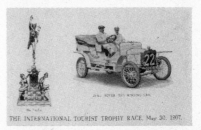

A commemorative card showing the
winner, a Rover car.

Bradford Walk to York in 1904, but the
Referee goes by car.

Waiting to set off for la Grande Chartreuse,
a superb Louis Levy photo, full of action
and detail.

No room on the top of the car! A
Manchester tram close-up (see Glossary
Appendix 2).

Fifth Avenue on Sunday Morning, with
New York's elite.

# RAILWAYS

The abundance and variety of railway postcards reflects the continuing interest in this form of transport since its inception in Britain. The period prior to 1923 is the most attractive, for then four major railway companies were formed to take over from the multitude of smaller companies which had existed previously.

Most of these smaller companies issued 'Official' postcards which usually included the company badge. The most prolific of all in the use of postcards was the London and North Western Railway Company and many millions were issued. The very early cards for the smaller companies command a considerable premium and this is one of the most specialist categories in the very wide field of cartology.

Perhaps even more popular than the collection of 'Official' cards, are the light railways running on narrow gauge lines. It has been a phenomenon of

*An early Irish Official railway correspondence card, with the reference number still pencilled at the top.*

*A pleasing Caledonian Railway official, with red back and seal.*

*These little motor trains in one unit were once quite popular; this card is made very collectable by its added timetable, which also fills half the space on the back.*

*The peculiar Lartigue Railway where the train was literally folded over a central tressle track (p/Lawrence).*

*An Australian train on exhibition, with a little postcard history attached (see text).*

*A commemorative for the centenary of the first French train.*

recent times to see a number of these lines revived and providing a considerable attraction by their continuing use of steam in a diesel and electric age. A spate of modern postcards can thus be added to the earlier ones which are now very expensive indeed.

What many collectors do not realise is the value of postcards which show the small branch lines which ran on standard gauge. Note the *illustration* of the small Great Northern Railway motor-train, running between Edgware and Finchley on the outskirts of London with time-table included, which continues in still greater detail on the reverse side.

Besides the ordinary railway, there are model and miniature railways, cliff lifts, funicular and mountain railways, pier railways and strange hybrids, like the Lartigue Railway of Ballybunion, County Kerry in Ireland, which ran on a single iron tressle track *(illustrated)*.

The Locomotive Publishing Company issued thousands of cards of railway trains and locomotives throughout the world. A series of twenty-four water colour drawings 'Expresses of the World', depicts some of the most famous lines, with an ever-changing scenic panorama, but the most splendid railway scenery is found on railway postcards of North America, Switzerland and India, with the famous Darjeeling Railway looping its way high up into the mountains. An unusual Australian train is *illustrated* and was exhibited to the public. The message explains that it was built in the Ipswich workshops, Queensland, and the carriages were made of Queensland timber. The message then continues "Charlie had to pay two guineas for the privilege of taking and selling postcards. I think we shall do very well. I have been at home all the week printing while he was out selling." Just another little bit of postcard history preserved for us.

## SHIPS AND INLAND WATERWAYS

In building a ship collection there are thousands of postcards available published by the shipping lines of the world. Here are a few of them you can look for, (the word 'Line' follows each name unless 'Co' is given):

| | | |
|---|---|---|
| Aberdeen | Dominion | Orient |
| Allan Royal Mail | Flushing | Orient-Pacific |
| American | General Steam | Orient-Royal Mail |
| Anchor | Navigation Co. | Pacific |
| Belfast Steamship | Hamburg-Amerika | Pacific Mail |
| Bibby | Henderson | P and O |
| Blue Anchor | Holland-America | Red Star |
| Blue Funnel | Imperial Direct West | Royal Mail Steam |
| Booth | Indies Mail Service Co. | Packet Co. |
| Bucknell Steamship | Japan Mail Steamship | Royal Netherlands |
| Cammell Laird | Co. (N.Y.K.) | West India Mail |
| Canadian Pacific | Lamport and Holt | Shaw Saville-Albion |
| Carron | Leyland | (R.M. Line) |
| City | Marseille Navigation | Swedish Lloyd |
| City of Dublin | Messageries Maritimes | Union Castle |
| Coast | New Zealand Shipping | Watson |
| Cunard | Co. | White Star |
| Cunard White Star | Norddeutscher Lloyd | Yeoward |
| Deutsche Ost-Africa | | |

The 'Official' cards usually carry some information showing that they were issued by the shipping company. On the reverse side you may find the flag or official badge or the words "On Board the . . . ", the name of the line with perhaps some advertising slogan, or the name of a shipping agent with details of frequency of sailing and routes followed. Most cards that are not official lack these details but carry instead the name of the postcard publisher.

The best cards fall into two categories. First the early chromo-litho vignettes and particularly those published by Andrew Reid and Company of Newcastle-upon-Tyne. Second, the poster and semi-poster cards which were the premier official advertising cards for the shipping companies. The menu card is a distinctive type quite widely used, which carried a poster card attached by perforations to the menu for the day. When you had finished your meal, if you had not already spilt your soup over it when the

A South Manchuria Railway Co., official, gilded and silvered, with the sail on the right deeply embossed.

An official shipping poster PMC combined with a Luncheon Menu, which has been detached from the lower edge; sgd/H. Cassiers.

The Golden Gate Ferry crossing the narrow channel that leads to San Francisco Bay, California.

A commemorative of the arrival in 1897 of the first shipment of gold from Alaska on board the ship Portland; the deck near the bows is gilded.

Canal collectors prize cards with plenty of barges on them–this one rates high with 14 waiting patiently; p/Downer, Watford.

A float for the Amalgamated Society of Watermen, Lightermen and Bargemen with five little boys enjoying themselves.

ship hit an unusually large wave, you could tear off the postcard and send it to one of your friends whilst keeping the menu as a memento. I imagine that one of the most difficult collections to complete would be a collection of menu postcards dated for every day in a particular year and an intrepid collector somewhere might like to try this.

This is only a beginning to the endless possibilities for a ship collection. There are cargo boats, coastal and river steamers, including many of the famous old paddle type (side and rear), Royal yachts, hospital ships, training ships, tugs, ferries, houseboats, yachts and fishing boats. All the facilities used can be brought in to build a fascinating picture of marine life. Docks and harbours, quayside scenes, fishermen and fish-markets, ship-building, shipyards and launching day. You can sail the Seven Seas, tour the Scottish lochs or the Great Lakes, or plunge into the history of ships by means of a set 200 cards long published in Holland.

An entirely separate category comes under the heading of 'Rescue Services', Starting with the wrecks themselves and including perhaps even the icebergs that may have caused them, this focuses our attention on the greatest wreck of all time—that of the giant liner Titanic in 1912. There are dozens of Titanic postcards, many of them faked, since they often represent her sister ship; the genuine ones are mostly good photographic types and I have one posted from Southampton on April 18th 1912, just three days after the catastrophe. Part of the message reads "No dear, it is no trouble to send papers, it is really heartbreaking, to see people here, everyone has either father, husband, brother or sweetheart on board". This associated message adds considerably to the value of such a card.

The lifeboat is the most sought-after rescue service postcard with good close-up photographic views top of the list. Then come lightships, warning bouys and lights, coastguard stations, coastguards and lighthouses. There is a Tuck oilette series entitled 'The Lifeboat at Work'.

With the revival of much of Britain's canal system, it is not surprising that canal postcards should also be popular. Good views of barges add to the value, especially if associated with a lock and some action in the scene. An unusual aspect of this theme is *illustrated,* a float for the Amalgamated Society of Watermen, Lightermen and Bargemen.

## MAPS AND EXPLORATION

Once again, the heyday of the picture postcard coincided with great progress, the famous race for the Poles, and there are many valuable cards often with expedition cachets and special postmarks. A very fine chromo-litho set of twelve cards epitomises the history of exploration, with the voyage of Marco Polo through Asia and the discovery of America by Christopher Columbus. Mountaineering expeditions were not forgotten and a set of eighteen cards commemorates the 1924 attempt to climb Mount Everest.

Our maps were produced because of the work of early explorers and so it is natural to include this subject here. Two extensive series (Bacon's and Walker's) cover most regions of the British Isles and are popular with many different types of collector. Naturally, every local collection needs a map or two to enhance its interest, but the railway enthusiast also wants to see the

*One of the earliest map postcards, for the Paris Pneumatic Post, 1882.*

*A special Tuck Souvenir Postcard showing the way to Raphael House, which was destroyed, along with all their records, in the blitz of 1940.*

*A rather humbling map for everyone living in Britain and Europe.*

*Map of World War One actions, one of six covering 24th August to 10th November 1914, published from* **The Bystander.**

course of railway lines which have long since ceased to exist. The Cyclists Touring Club issued a series of maps with routes for cyclists and there are maps for the Boer War, the Russo-Japanese War and many covering World War I. Some are specialist types, like those linked with the activities of the Navy, with an inset picture of a battleship or cruiser.

An interesting series of colour maps covers most continents of the world and advertises Remy with one or two small pictures added, representative of the area on the map. Exploration is once again tied in, with the one for the Belgian Congo depicting an explorer and his natives trekking through the jungle and crossing mysterious rivers. An embossed series of the continents is full of detail and distinguished by a gilt border. One of my favourite maps gives every detail of the islands of the Great Barrier Reef off the coast of Queensland, Australia. Talking of Australia, just look at its size on the postcard *illustrated* when superimposed on the European continent. It quite takes the breath away!

One of the very earliest map postcards is also *reproduced*, dated 1882, and shows a simple plan of Paris that was used in connection with the pneumatic post of the telegraphic department, which conveyed containers along pneumatic tubes by use of air pressure. Britain tried a similar system but had abandoned it by then.

There are also maps of towns and cities, comic and romantic maps, particularly of the Isle of Arran, lake and mountain charts, and a set of six Tuck cards, covering central London. Tuck's own Raphael House and its location *illustrated,* is a map card prized by collectors.

# 12 New Collecting Themes and Ideas

Having surveyed the tremendously wide field covered by picture postcards, you may have already decided on certain 'straight' themes you will pursue. But you may be more confused than ever, or just want to be different, finding a theme that interests you and yet cuts across all the conventional ones, perhaps allowing you to assemble an interesting cross-section of all kinds of cards.

Here are just a few ideas you could choose from, and as we discuss most of them it may help you to see how you can think up dozens more:

| | |
|---|---|
| Frontier Posts | Moving Houses and Disappearing Homes |
| Strange! | Striking Figure Clocks |
| Graffiti | What the Camera Saw |
| Mount Vesuvius | Ancient Ceremonies and Customs |
| Lychgates | Weathering the Weather |
| Gretna Green | Tollhouses and Bridges |
| Early Telephones | Walking Round the World |
| British Islands | Unusual Transport |
| Queer Bridges | Puzzles and Riddles |
| The Cake Walk | The Artist in Action |
| Record Beaters | The Loch Ness Monster |
| Village Pumps | On Top of the World |
| Numbered Cards | Model Villages and Buildings |
| Scottish Castles | Matchbox Labels |
| Street Lights | Homes and Houses |
| Famous Trees | Ceremonial Archways |
| The Oldest . . . | The Last . . . |
| Hansom Cabs | Jacob's Ladderways |
| Old Inn Signs | Beautiful Waterfalls |
| Bathing Machines | Old Timbered Houses |
| Sand Modelling | Early Car Breakdowns |

A few brief notes about most of these will give you ideas for developing a small theme, although some of them have almost limitless possibilities.

**Frontier Posts:**
Soldiers in different national uniforms, sometimes with barriers across the road and stones inscribed with the frontier name. There are more of these cards than you would expect.

**Moving Houses and Disappearing Homes:**
Houses that were taken down and re-erected elsewhere, such as the fifteenth century Crosby Hall, moved from Bishopsgate, London in 1905, and re-erected in Chelsea. The Old House in Hereford, moved literally without having to take it down. Cottages and houses in Lynmouth, North Devon swept away by floods in 1952. The earth slip in Northwich, Cheshire in 1901 and 1909.

## Strange!

Siamese Twins and Bohemian Twins, their inseparable lives. Two lads in a narrow French street wearing dustbin lids as hats. The Cunard liner Queen Mary straddling Trafalgar Square (to illustrate its size). Man seated on a beer barrel parachuting to the ground under an even larger beer barrel. Plenty of fantasy cards would fit this heading.

## Striking Figure Clocks:

Not such a small theme as you would think! One in Wells Cathedral; Matthew the Miller Clock in Exeter, and a famous one that stood near Bow Church, London until 1929, when it was bought by Henry Ford and taken to Detroit in 1930. Perkeo in Heidelberg, Germany.

## Graffiti:

Yes, those wall paintings are not new. Best conveyed by looking at the *illustration* showing boys throwing snowballs at a little World War I figure.

## What the Camera Saw:

An endless subject, not only including pictures of the early box-like cameras but a selection of early photographs taken by private individuals. One I have is a superb close-up photograph and the message on the back reads, "This is a genuine spot in our garden, a sparrow's nest, two young birds and one egg yet to hatch". All very clear in the picture.

## Mount Vesuvius:

There are postcards of eruptions in 1872 and 1895, a number of fine advertising cards issued by Thomas Cook and Son, close-up pictures of the funicular railway, and many views taken from the Bay of Naples.

## Ancient Ceremonies and Customs:

Another subject with wide possibilities. From the ancient Tynwald ceremony on the Isle of Man to the Dunmow Flitch, and from Town Criers to the blowing of the Ripon Horn every evening at nine o'clock. An unusual one concerns Rye Harbour, one of the cinque ports, and shows a faculty case being held in the Church before the Chancellor, Dr. Tristam. You can include such events as the pelting with eggs of two men fixed in the stocks, and the shells scattered all round.

## Weathering the Weather:

Thunderstorms, the frozen sea at Southend in 1905, a record Australian heat wave in 1939, seasons of the year, several comic weather forecast series, the fisherman's storm warning fixed in a monument at Dunbar, Scotland, and a commemorative card for the inventor of the barometer, *(illustrated)*.

## Gretna Green:

The famous runaway marriage parlour, its original history, famous marriage certificates, such as Lord Erskine's and Lord Drumlanrig, newspaper cuttings, pictures galore of the exterior and interior, a wedding in progress, the famous John Peel married there in 1797 *(illustrated);* six stages of a runaway wedding showing a chase in progress, a card autographed by Richard Rennison, holding his records of over 2,000 marriages in seven years, and finally the Gretna Green Railway disaster of the 22nd May 1915.

**Early Telephones:**
Mostly comic and romantic cards, but many unusual angles such as the field telephone in World War I and the fast disappearing telegraph poles.

**Walking Round the World:**
Once a popular pastime and a number of such walkers financed their journey by selling postcards depicting their attempt. The *illustrated* card of the champion tramp offers to give you a good square meal if you present this card, should you meet him, that is "If I am not dead-broke myself".

**British Islands:**
Hundreds of these appear on picture postcards and if you wish you can include man-made ones, such as Spithead Fort, outside Portsmouth Harbour *(illustrated)* F. G. O. Stuart 1605. Goes well with a collection of island Cinderella stamps.

**Unusual Transport:**
Many less expensive foreign cards could be used in this collection. Then there are the transporter bridges (the car of one of these is *illustrated*), the sea car, which was used at Brighton and St. Malo, the sand-yacht *(illustrated)*, and the Spanish Aero-car at Niagara Falls.

**Puzzles and Riddles:**
A truly open-ended subject. What do you make of the card *illustrated*, which is dominated by 12.12.12. A clue appears on the stones below, yes, it's the date. But when you stop and think, there are very few dates in a century when the day, month and year are the same. There is the puzzle epitaph at Christchurch Priory, the card with five different views of the same man, cleverly taken by using four mirrors. An entertaining subject.

*An excellent example of graffiti, a theme which reaches back into ancient times.*

*The Weather theme–a card commemorating the inventor of the barometer, Torricelli, who was a pupil of the famous Galileo.*

*Almost a legendary character, John Peel is best known for his hunting song, but his marriage at Gretna Green just adds to the legend.*

*Autographed 'A No. 1 The Rambler' the back of this card is entitled 'Meal Ticket' and also advertises a book about his adventures.*

*This island fort is complete with lighthouse, signal station and landing stage.*

*The Rouen transporter car, which hung 140 feet below the span, ready to cross the River Seine. The bridge was blown up in 1940.*

*Sand-yachting is not new, although it has recently become popular again.*

*A card to puzzle your friends; note the other dates on the stones, which could also include 10.10.10.*

### The Cake-Walk:

With children doing it, even animals doing it, one French set of ten cards illustrates each individual step. There is even a card advertising 'Allan's Cake-Walk Album, price one shilling'. For those not sure of what constitutes the cake-walk, it was of American-Negro origin and a slab of cake was awarded to those thinking up the most aristocratic figures and steps.

### The Artist in Action:

The world of easels, brushes and paints, with a number of series using the easel or the artist's palette as a frame for the picture. Many artists at work can be found on postcards. I have a fine scene at Chiddingstone, Kent, with the artist in the foreground just completing a large canvas, if one only knew who he was? You can include the homes and haunts of artists like Constable, and specimens of their work.

### Record Beaters:

Such as the billiard match in London, where a world record break of 1,143 was achieved by the Australian, George Gray. Or a picture of Epsom's tradesman, Mr. Dearle, returning in his carriage from his 80th Derby. Then the failures can be included, such as the card autographed by Fred H. Grubb, showing him poised on his racing cycle, in which he says, "Am going for record again later in season" (dated May 1913).

### Loch Ness Monster:

Many hilarious cards of course, but some serious ones, such as the authentic photograph taken by a London surgeon on the 19th April 1934.

**Village Pumps:**

Now almost a thing of the past. This can be widened to horse drinking troughs, fountains and wells.

**On Top of the World:**

Groups on mountain summits; exclusive guide card for Snaefell, Isle of Man, with a diamond cachet on the back if possible, or the top of the Eiffel Tower, the view from the Bridgewater Monument in Hertfordshire, or from one of the look-out towers on the continent, such as Schöpfel, in Austria. You can add ways of getting there too, like the Abraham's card *illustrated,* 'Motor cycling in Lakeland'.(642).

**Numbered Cards:**

The number was stamped on and they indicate a limited issue or a claim to prizes given by firms like Symingtons. The Benvenuto Cellini Commemorative issued in 1900 was limited to 1,000 cards. During World War I, the winning numbers from a batch of postcards issued in aid of the Blinded Soldiers' Childrens' Fund were flashed on the screen of a cinema in the East End of London, and each winner received a £1 war savings certificate. Even your order for oysters in a New Orleans restaurant entitled you to a numbered postcard *(illustrated).*

**Model Villages and Buildings:**

Another fascinating subject ranging from a model of the Lord Mayor's Show in 1616 to the villages of Wimbourne Minster, Bekonscot, Beaconsfield and Bourton-on-the-Water. There is old London Bridge,

*An appliquéd thin wooden palette painted in oils is a nice addition to an artist theme; it also shows you how to slot cards into an old album in the correct manner (see Ch. 13).*

*A rough ride to the top; an imaginative photograph by Abrahams which could also find a place in a motor-cycle collection.*

*Is this Restaurant still in business, and are numbered postcards in use too ? If so, I wonder what the latest number is?*

*Match-box cards are not easy to find; this interesting example features types used in India.*

Stonehenge, a steam-driven fair roundabout, John Lister's midget town at the Paris exhibition, Heath Robinson's 'Ideal Home', the Queen's Dolls' House and the mole at Zeebrugge in the First World War. One of the finest model collections was made by Richard Old (1856–1932), which went on many travelling exhibitions. You can find postcards from it of Milan and Ulm Cathedrals, and other buildings to scale containing as many as eight thousand pieces.

## Scottish Castles:

Just one branch of what would otherwise be a ten-thousand card castle collection. Distinguish here the specialised type of Scottish Castle, the fortified house, the four-square keep, a simple tower house, the turreted tower house and the larger castles built round a central courtyard.

## Street Lights:

What a variety of types here! One even has the names of the streets in Sheffield painted over the gas-lamp. Those outside shops carried advertisements, another surmounts the railings around the Dick Whittington Stone on Highgate Hill in London *(illustrated)*, while some highly ornamented lanterns illuminate the entrance to Monte Carlo Casino. Picture the lamplighter or the lamp cleaner, climbing an exceedingly tall pair of steps, outside the cafe Americain in Paris, as a horse-bus gallops past!

## Homes and Houses:

Thousands of pictures were taken and unhappily carry no captions to help us in locating them. You can bring these together into a fine collection illustrating every possible form of architecture. There are postcards used by estate agents to advertise homes for sale, which carry a detailed description on the back, and those advertising new estates which show a plan of the ground and first floors. In Eastbourne, a picture of your house could be set alongside multi-views of the resort.

## Ceremonial Archways:

These were once very popular and were used to welcome Royalty or in celebration of a special occasion. There is the bedstead arch, the Browns' Bridge arch in symbol of Britain's defence, and the cycle trades' arch fitted with Lucas lamps and bells.

## The Oldest:

Which ranges from the oldest bridge in England, at Waltham Abbey (1066), to the oldest municipal fire brigade, that of Edinburgh. You will be able to sort out the rival claims to the oldest inhabited house in the country, Ye Olde Round House, St. Alban's, or the Jews House, Lincoln.

## The Last . . .:

The last bus, the last tram, the last train, are well known comic cards, but more serious subjects include the last day's work by oxen at Saddlescombe in Sussex. Ye Olde Trip to Jerusalem Inn in Nottingham not only lays claim to being the last stop in England before the Crusaders left for Jerusalem but it also has a place in our previous collection as the oldest home-brewed house in England.

## Hansom Cabs:

Joseph Hansom designed this vehicle in 1834 with its especially large

*The interesting ornamental lamp above the Dick Whittington stone on Highgate Hill in North London.*

*Hansom cab driver falls for handsome fare!*

*The Boston tea-party was linked with this old sign, above the (then) Fenchurch Street, London, house that supplied the tea.*

*Another example of a close-up, a nice addition to a collection of Edwardian Bathing Machines.*

*A private action photo like this, with the story on the other side, is almost the most interesting type of card to find; taken near Dunstable, Bedfordshire.*

wheels to prevent it overturning. You can find plenty of street scenes featuring these cabs, some nice close-ups and even some comic cards, like the set of four 'Une Aventure Galante', which tells the story of the lady cab-driver who fell victim (literally) to the charm of her passenger *(illustrated)*.

### Jacob's Ladderways:
Those long flights of steps which exist in more places than one realises. Try counting the number of steps on each postcard but don't go cross-eyed in the process. Which flight has the greatest number of steps? (See full article in *Picture Post Card Monthly*, July, 1982).

### Old Inn Signs:
Tuck issued a series 'Old London Signs', (Art Series 1196) and there is at least one other anonymous set of six. There are innumerable close-ups such as 'The Five Alls', at Marlborough, the 'Cat and Fiddle' and 'The Olde Trusty Servante', both in the New Forest, and 'The Cat and Fiddle' at Buxton.

### Bathing Machines:

This needs to be a selected theme, perhaps just including the different types, the advertisements they carried, amusing incidents connected with them, and of course, close-ups such as the one *illustrated*.

### Old Timbered Houses:

Some of the famous early houses with timber frames, a theme for those who like the picturesque. Many have now been pulled down and this adds to the interest in this subject.

### Sand-Modelling:

Figures and scenes were sculptured in sand, and competitions were held and attracted considerable interest. One card shows the judging in progress with a large crowd behind. Many very professional models were made, such as 'The Fortune of War' and 'The Last Message'.

### Early Car Breakdowns:

These were frequent and they have not escaped the postcard photographer. You can find cars on tow, vehicles being pushed and comic cards of all descriptions. One card tells of a patent inner tube on trial that let the family down and Harold writes, "just a momentum (!!) of our fine trip to Sheffield, with a bad start, a bad middle but a safe return. Father here is doing a great deal toward tyring himself." The very fine picture shows the father and the chauffeur at work *(illustrated)*. You could tie in with this an advertisement card for one of these tyres.

Although only one or two of these themes may interest you personally, I hope that my purpose in discussing them has been achieved, namely, that you can see the coverage given by postcards is so wide and so varied that you can tailor-make a collection to your exact interests and to your pocket. From time to time, it is said that postcards are becoming too expensive, but if collectors *will* limit their interest to a few subjects much collected by everyone else as well, then it is no wonder that the prices of those cards continue to rise. There is no shortage of cards as an appendix to this book fully establishes. So find some themes that few people have thought about.

With a little research you could build a fine collection of under one hundred cards, so specialised that it is unique, yet its cost might be very small.

Why not even make a single postcard collection! Yes, a story on a single postcard can be quite intriguing. For example, an embossed map-card issued after the opening of the Panama Canal, shows the route in great detail, its length (forty miles), time taken to travel through, number of men employed and estimated total cost, the functioning of the three great locks, the levels of the different oceans and the time saved from a selection of places. From New York by sea to Panama was cut from 11,977 miles to 1,957 miles.

Not only is the picture postcard hobby entertaining and interesting, it also can be very educational.

# 13   Spending Your Money Wisely

In these days of high inflation and soaring prices it becomes very difficult to maintain proper values. We have to constantly adjust our viewpoint and because postcard collecting has only recently been re-discovered and has enjoyed a sudden boom, the market is very volatile. As few people have money to waste, spending it wisely is most important, and time used in weighing up the factors involved will be well repaid.

Many postcard catalogues are now available; three in Britain, three in Italy and a number of specialised ones, especially in the United States. Two French catalogues have reached a very good standard and the French scene is probably more advanced than most. The British catalogues are still seeking a balanced presentation and consistency of valuation. So, if you spend a reasonable amount of money on postcards in any one year, it will pay you to obtain all the catalogues and thoroughly study the sections you are especially interested in. When prices vary so much, you could well save yourself twenty percent of your total spending.

There are now many regular postcard fairs held in different parts of the world and some particularly outstanding events, such as BIPEX (British International Postcard Exhibition) held in London for four days each September; the Hotel George V Fair in Paris, France (usually each April), and in New York, the International Post Card Bourse held for three days each May.

When you have attended one or two of these fairs, you will quickly come to appreciate that there is no shortage of postcards throughout the world. This has been a fear expressed by many collectors who may have read about the estimate often given of thirty-five million postcards still surviving today. That this must be a gigantic underestimate will be evident from an appendix to this book. But, although a very large number of cards still survive, this is not to say that the ones you particularly wish to collect are easily obtainable. Bearing in mind that the original number of different designs is colossal, the competition between early card publishers was so intense that they were always thinking about new and better designs, and they quickly dropped any that didn't sell well, however attractive they may have been.

So, you have to make a difficult decision when you see a card you particularly want and the price is very high. You may see it again quite soon at half the price, but it may be rare and this might be your opportunity. Unlike postage stamps and coins, with a few exceptions we still do not know which cards are only scarce and which are really rare. A dealer is in a better position to guess this, and he may well have already bought that card from another dealer and doubled the price. If he is well informed, he may be right but there are many dealers, unfortunately, who either ignorantly or deliberately charge very high prices for very common cards. There is therefore no substitute for acquiring as much knowledge as you can about the theme that interests you.

## POSTCARD AUCTIONS

There are now many postcard auctions where you can purchase cards in small or large lots. Some of these are run by local, national and international auction houses, who deal with a wide range of other antiques and collectables. Some are specialised postcard auctions only. In the United States, many of these are postal auctions due to the greater distances involved. The key to successful postal buying is careful comparison of estimated prices across a range of such auctions.

If you are bidding in a postal auction, you just have to decide on the figure you will pay for a particular lot and there are usually two main factors involved. If you particularly want a card or set of cards, you have to decide how high you will need to go to beat the unknown competition, since you cannot normally put in a 'buy bid'. On the other hand, you may aim for the opposite end of the spectrum, entering the lowest bids you think likely to obtain a reasonable proportion of the lots you are interested in. But do not put in foolish bids of, say, under half the estimated value. These only waste everyone's time, and your own postage.

This method certainly ensures you spend your money wisely providing that the condition of the cards you are bidding for has been made clear, and reputable postcard auctions will do this. The question of condition is therefore a most important factor in a postal auction where you probably have not had an opportunity to view the cards. You must also be certain that you understand the description and know that the cards are the ones you want. Frequently, customers have found that their purchases were quite different from what they had imagined. So, read the listings carefully and don't jump to hasty conclusions.

If you are present at a large auction, the danger is that you will be carried away in the heat of the moment by the desire to obtain particular lots, and then afterwards you ruefully admit to other collectors and dealers "I paid too much for these!"

This is why auction realisations need careful study and an appreciation of the factors behind them. One auction may be well attended because it is well advertised or falls at a suitable time. High prices may be realised. Another may be poorly attended because it is out of season and poorly advertised, or there may be such a surfeit of material available that it forces all the prices down. If you alone wish to obtain a lot you may get it at a good price, but suppose there is just one other person like you who particularly wants it, you may bid against each other and not only push the price to a new record but perhaps far beyond its real value. Any dealer that happens to possess that same card at the time will then probably put his price up to correspond, even though only two people really wanted it and no one else was interested.

So here are a few suggested rules you can apply at auctions if you wish to spend your money wisely:
1. Set a figure for each lot you wish to buy and don't be moved by emotion to exceed that figure.

2. Never buy 'blind'; that means without either inspecting the lot if all cards are not described, or knowing their condition whether actually seen or assessed by the auctioneers. (At a recent London sale, three Queen Victoria Jubilee cards were sold to a dealer at about the current price but two of them were in a terrible condition. The original description by a top international auction house purported to give condition but failed to properly do so. Two of them re-appeared soon after in another auction catalogue where the descriptions were better but still misleading enough to leave two very disillusioned buyers.)
3. Don't rely on any price estimate unless you know for certain that the auctioneer knows his cards and gives fair estimates. (The name of an international auctioneer is no guarantee that they understand postcards. In fact, only one of the top London auction houses at present gets anywhere near a right valuation).
4. You generally reap what you sow. Results are usually compatible with time spent in viewing the lots. Buy in haste and you may sell at a loss.
5. In estimating larger lots avoid too much 'averaging', which really means that you try to *guess* the average value of all the cards in the lot; unless you know you are good at doing this, don't try it.
6. If you buy a large collection in order to obtain a few cards you want you should expect to pay roughly what a dealer would pay, bearing in mind that you will probably have to sell the rest of the collection to a dealer.
7. If someone approaches you and asks you not to bid against them for a particular lot, take no notice of them—that is illegal.
8. Always bid clearly; the idea that an auctioneer is miraculously programmed to your slightest wink or merest finger twitch is quite untrue. They can be very alert but they don't possess all-seeing eyes. Raising your catalogue in a clear gesture is the method preferred by many auctioneers.

## SELLING YOUR CARDS

Even the new collector has to think about selling his cards, although he may have no intention of doing so when he buys them. Your circumstances may change and force you to sell, your interest may suddenly evaporate or you may desire to instruct your heirs as to their disposal. So, this aspect is just the last and most crucial one in your investment chain. You may, of course, decide to leave your collection to the local library or museum, or your family may take enough interest for you to know that they will take good care of it.

The usual question asked is, "Shall I sell my collection to a dealer or place it in an auction?" Let us consider carefully what these alternatives mean.

If you want a quick sale you will probably have to sell to a dealer, but if time is not against you, you can place it more carefully. Obviously, if you could find another collector who will buy direct from you, he would give you the best price, or you may be able to make up a list and sell the collection piecemeal. The problem here is that the best cards will sell readily and you will be left with the poor ones which even a dealer will not want. If you try an advertisement, you must balance the cost of this against the possible improved realisation.

As you purchased your cards, you probably came to know some reliable dealers. This does not necessarily mean those from whom you purchased cards at the cheapest prices, as they may make the lowest offer for your collection. Unfortunately, however, some of the more expensive dealers may still only offer you a ridiculous price. Certainly, you should ask several dealers to give you their offer, and not allow them to force you into saying what you want for them. However certain you may be of their value, dealers are aware that usually people fall into three categories:

1. They have absolutely no idea how valuable their cards are.
2. They have a greatly inflated idea of their value.
3. They really know the value because of the knowledge and experience they have gained. Let's hope that in time you will fall into the third group.

Beware of the dealer who offers you a price, and when you say that you would like to have another opinion before you decide, tells you that he won't be able to keep his offer open, and that he can assure you it is the best offer you will get. Usually his price is too low to stand competition from another reputable dealer.

Suppose all this puts you right off dealers, and you decide it will be best to go to an auction house. A specialised postcard auctioneer may well split up your collection into numerous small lots and thus obtain the best prices for you, but you have to weigh this against a fairly high commission rate; anything from 7½% to 20%. You may feel that you will get the best deal by going to a well-known international house where they may not split up your collection but will sell it for perhaps 10% commission (where they may also charge the buyer 10% commission). So, what are the problems here? Judging the best time of year to sell is the first point to consider. Allowing for two or three months for auction preparation, the Autumn or early Winter is a good time, although an auction in mid-December often fails to attract high prices. Certainly the Summer is better avoided if possible, when people are interested in outdoor events and holidays.

Try to make sure that you go to an auctioneer who will give a reasonable description of your collection, even where postcards are sold in fairly large lots. A discerning auctioneer will still take out the better cards and offer them separately, with the appropriate description. I have frequently purchased scarce or rare cards of considerable value not mentioned in descriptions and which often no one else had noticed. Having done all you can, it is still a gamble as to whether you realise the full value of your collection. At most auctions, some lots go to very high figures often far exceeding the true value and you would be very pleased with the result. At the same auction other items will fall flat for lack of bidders.

It can also depend on the auctioneer for a particular sale. The alert experienced auctioneer never misses a bid, knows the pace to go and draws the bidders by casual remarks and proper pausing at the right time. The alert dealer knows that he can get bargains when the auctioneer goes too fast for most bidders in the room.

At a well-known international auction house recently, the auctioneer was far too quick on the hammer and so failed in the first essential of an auctioneer, an understanding of bidding psychology. He missed a number of bids and when he was challenged on one of these, quite justly, I believe, he did not give the bidder the benefit of the doubt, and refused to re-open it. I happened to be the under bidder and so obtained the very choice lot at three-quarters of the price it should have sold for. I felt very sorry for the vendor of some exceedingly fine cards. At the same auction, I purchased a unique collection for one-quarter of the price I was willing to pay, simply because no-one else appeared to be interested. Here the auctioneer was in no way at fault nor was the catalogue description. True, the estimate was well under what it should have been, but the result could only be put down to inexperience by many dealers, and shortage of cash that particular day. That sort of collection is hard to find at the best of times. The vendor would undoubtedly have found a good price by shopping around, and would have saved his auction commission.

This will perhaps give you some insight into the pros and cons of auctions. Generally speaking I can buy more soundly at auctions than privately, because when a collection is brought to me, I have to pay according to its true value. At most auctions, by careful bidding I can obtain much greater value for the money paid. At those same auctions however, many other dealers will pay very much more for some collections than I would ever do. As an accountant, I am one of the very few dealers in Britain operating a proper costing system which ensures that I meet the overall profit margins I have set myself. I therefore put much emphasis upon careful buying.

So to what conclusion can you come if you want to sell your cards. These basic principles apply:
1. There is no substitute for really knowing your cards and their value.
2. When you want to sell don't rush at it but get estimates from at least three dealers.
3. If you have good cards and scarce ones, it may be best to auction them. Study carefully auctioneers' methods and procedure before making a choice, and choose the right time of year.
4. Tell the auctioneer in writing about your good cards; you can then question his description when you receive your vendor's catalogue and withdraw them if you feel he has not done them justice. If he has failed to carry out your instructions, you should be able to contest successfully any cancellation fee.

## TAXATION PROBLEMS

This varies from country to country, so it is only possible to give a few general principles, coupled with some idea of what happens in the United Kingdom.

There is often an exemption allowance covering the disposal of 'chattels', that is movable property, which would include picture postcards. Where this is, say, £2,000 in value for each item then even a large collection could be sold without having to worry about any Capital Gains Tax or similar labelled taxes. There is one important exception to this, however, and that is where cards belong to one 'set'. So if you decide to buy a complete set of twelve Mucha 'Months of the Year' (Le Mois), or one of the longer sets such as 'Collection des Cent', it will be worth pausing to remember that on disposal they are aggregated in value, and would attract tax if adding up to more than £2,000 for the set. There is something to be said for not having a complete set after all! Of course, many postcards have not reached anything like such figures, but when it is realised how much they have appreciated in value over the last ten years or so, it is as well to think about this matter when acquiring them, for that is when you may saddle yourself with the problem. You should keep bills or invoices for such expensive cards, for you may need to prove how much they cost, since Capital Gains Tax is calculated on the gain on disposal over original cost, if acquired after 6th April, 1965. If acquired before that date, only the gain (or loss) attributable to the period since then is subject to tax.

The other matter often forgotten, is where one becomes a 'dealer' in postcards, perhaps just on a small scale, or part-time. So long as a collector merely disposes of his cards to a fellow collector by way of exchange then he is not dealing for money. But if you buy cards *with the purpose* of selling them again for profit, then you are trading, and your earnings would be subject to taxation. That does not mean you cannot buy cards and build up a collection which you hope to dispose of *eventually* at a profit. That is different from *trading* in postcards.

The most difficult aspect of trading is where a dealer, whether part-time or full-time, is also a collector. Unless you are careful about your records, you could find a problem arises either when you eventually dispose of your business, or when you dispose of your personal collection. In your business records you must not enter as purchases any cards which you keep for yourself. That is not as difficult as it sounds; I just show the full total I have paid out in my cash book, but in my stock book I only record the proportion going into stock, and the difference is clearly marked as 'own collection'. This way there is no question as to values of acquisition if I sell my business, but do not sell my own collection.

Many countries also operate a Sales Tax, sometimes just applicable to transactions within one state, as with some of the United States. In Britain this is called Value Added Tax, and is meant to tax the difference between cost of acquisition and sale. Unfortunately this is not true of postcards, for often there is no VAT on them when purchased at an auction, so the full amount (15% at present) is borne on the profit margin only. So far all protests have failed to iron out this extremely unfair situation, made worse by the large number of part-time dealers who trade below the minimum threshold for registration for VAT, but charge around the same prices as those dealers paying this extra tax. If you exceed the threshold figure, you must register, but many dealers find it better to restrict their sales in each Financial Year to below that threshold. Otherwise, you might need to increase your turnover each year by as much as £10,000 to pay for the tax, with no extra net benefit at all.

## STORING YOUR COLLECTION

Finally, it would be to no avail if we spent our money wisely, but failed to look after our collection properly. It should not be necessary to warn collectors never to leave their cards in a room or basement that is damp. If this happens, the layers of card will gradually separate, or tiny rust marks called 'foxing' will quickly lower their value.

Many collectors use the better condition early albums for storing their less valuable cards, and that is fine providing you are careful in putting cards in and taking them out. There are usually four corner diagonal 'tabs' formed from slanting cuts in the stout paper or card. Gently place one side of the postcard through the two slots, *under* the tab, and back through the next slot. Then place the opposite two corners *over* the tabs so that just the corners go through the far slots (see *illustration*). You only damage cards if you try to force all four corners *under* all the tabs. When properly inserted as described above, the card on the reverse side will go the opposite way round, to form an *under* and *over* for each pair of corners.

There are now many modern albums in which you can keep the better cards, but just check when buying them that the material used does not cause any chemical reaction with photographic cards. The other widely used form of storing facility is the 'shoe-box' or similar shaped box, often purpose-built, just as they were by many manufacturers more than seventy years ago. Dividers can be inserted, and cards kept in individual transparent wrappers.

When you pick cards up, never hold them just close to their corners, and if you flip quickly through a pack of postcards, be careful to do so gently, not bending them in the middle. Many marks on cards can be removed by use of the *right* kind of rubber, and album indentations can be gently ironed out, but never with a too-hot iron directly onto the card, unless you collect cinderrellas! With experience and care, you can build a collection you will be proud to show to your friends, and exhibit at postcard fairs.

# 14 How to Increase Your Knowledge

What does that old adage mean—a little knowledge is a dangerous thing? With certain things a little knowledge is sufficient for what we need. But if after gaining a little knowledge about postcards, we think we then know it all, or can guess the rest, that is where it can be dangerous. Often it is the attitude of mind that is important.

So from the beginning—now—decide what you want to do with postcards. If you just want to collect a few topographicals, or use postcards to illustrate other collections, then you can get by with the minimum of knowledge. But if you want to use the hobby to the full, or even just make a reasonable collection as an investment, it is worth extending your knowledge. No doubt about it, you will reap dividends both in interest and financially by reading all you can. So let us examine some books that are worth reading.

Those here recommended cover the subject, or certain aspects of it, fairly thoroughly, and have all established a reputation for the information they contain. There are many others, some of them specialising in one special theme or type of postcard, and it is not the part of an introduction to the subject to deal with those. You will find extensive bibliographies in many of the following books to tell you about them.

**Pictures in the Post,** by Richard Carline, 1959, 2nd edition 1971, Gordon Fraser, London.

Traces the postcard as an art form, and its early origins. Strong in the early growth period, including the illustrated envelope. Well-researched from contemporary sources, with interesting information on some outstanding artists. Written in an easy style, with fine illustrations, many of the cards being very scarce, and some rare. Good documentation, an index, and a bibliography containing lots of unusual sources. In many English libraries, and still obtainable recently in the United States. 128 large pages.

**The Picture Postcard and its Origins,** by Frank Staff, 1966, 2nd edition 1979, Lutterworth Press, London.

Although this covers some of the ground dealt with by the previous book, it complements rather than duplicates it. Between them these two give the best description of the Victorian scene. Again very readable, with well chosen illustrations, including much related ephemera and many rare cards. If one had a criticism it is in the choice of title which should more correctly read 'The Origins of the Picture Postcard', for the first 43 of the 81 text pages refer to the pre-postcard period. Index, but only brief bibliography. 96 large pages.

**Pioneer Postcards,** by Jefferson R. Burdick, 1957, reprinted with note *c.*1965, Nostalgia Press, New York.

This is really an outstanding check list of all early cards up to 1898, with many of them illustrated. Strong in cards of the U.S.A., it does give a number of early European ones too. It is indispensable for the collector of early cards, and is a fine piece of research which is being updated for a new edition, hopefully in the near future. Very difficult to find in Britain, 200 pages.

**Picture Postcards of the Golden Age,** Tonie and Valmai Holt, 1971, re-issued 1978, Postcard Publishing Co. London.

Called 'A Collector's Guide' this was the first book to really give a comprehensive account of what you could find in all categories and subject themes. It is packed with information, and deals *with* the cards rather than *about* them. Particularly strong in dealing with advertisements, the First World War, politics and portraits, or the human interest, but poor on ships and railway. You cannot do without this book if you collect subject cards. It is perhaps unfortunate that it was not revised for the 1978 re-issue, as some parts are badly out of date. Good index, 214 pages.

**Picture Postcards in the United States 1893-1918,** by George and Dorothy Miller, 1976, C. N. Potter Inc., New York.

This is one of the very best postcard books ever to have been issued, and should be in the possession of every postcard collector, even outside the United States. Obviously it devotes its pages to cards of that country, but its comprehensive coverage of sets issued, in particular gives it a much wider appeal. Many artists are dealt with, and there is a long section on exhibition cards. Advertising, social history, political and patriotic themes are also prominent. Index and select bibliography. 280 large pages. Being reprinted as a paperback.

**Picture Postcards and Their Publishers,** by Anthony Byatt, 1978, Golden Age Postcard Books, Malvern, Worcs.

This book by the present author won the Desmond Chamberlain Challenge Cup for Postcard Research for the year 1978/1979. Although it is set out in publisher order, its range is far wider, covering every conceivable theme, and the seven detailed indexes enable you to find the information you want very quickly. You can sort out trade marks, publishers and artists' names and initials, sets, subjects, as well as much history of the postcard, including a year by year synopsis of the best cards issued by the famous house of Tuck. Illustrations are chosen to be representative, rather than of scarce or rare cards. There are some check lists, a map and pictures of notable trade marks. 391 pages covering more than 275 outstanding publishers.

**The American Postcard Guide to Tuck,** by Sally S. Carver, 1976, Carves Cards, Brookline, Mass. U.S.A.

This oblong paperback shows almost the entire range of Tuck cards on each right-hand page, with a potted description of them on each left-hand page. Each pair of pages is devoted to a different theme or subject. As it deals especially with American Tuck cards it includes Halloween, Thanksgiving, blacks, Indians, and Santa Claus—a firm favourite in the

U.S.A. So it does miss many productions by Tuck, England, but is still very comprehensive. 76 pages.

**Collecting Postcards in Colour, 1894-1914,** by William Duval and Valerie Monahan, 1978, Blandford Press, Poole, Dorset.

This book and the next are part of a lengthy series on all sorts of subjects, and is especially valuable for the 64 pages of illustrations in full colour with three cards to each page. The introductory chapters give a readable summary of the most interesting features of postcard history and collecting subjects, although there are a number of factual errors. For example, the Tuck 'Oilette' process was not established by the turn of the century, but was first introduced in 1903. The value rating marks are often quite erroneous, particularly for the top categories, and the use of a triple 'rarity' mark is most misleading. But if you want to get to know what many of the better cards look like, the colour photography alone makes this book worthwhile. 212 pages.

**Collecting Postcards in Colour, 1914-1930,** by Valerie Monahan, 1980, uniform with above.

Again with 64 pages of illustrations, but only 48 pages in colour. This period includes the cards of World War One, and the type known as Art Deco. The introductory chapters deal with the war, social history, some best-selling series, especially children's cards which enjoyed a boom then, and details of many less-well-known artists. It is good to note that the top RRR marking is used with much greater restraint. A list of postcard clubs in Gt. Britain and the U.S.A., together with dealers, catalogues, and periodicals makes a valuable appendix, although this information quickly gets out of date. 176 pages.

**Picture Postcards and Travel,** by Frank Staff, 1979, Lutterworth Press, London.

Although bordering on the specialist side, travel touches so many fields that I have included this book here. Like his other book, the very careful choice of fine cards makes the illustrations outstanding, and the printing adds to this. Because he is a lifelong collector, Frank's cards are never ordinary, and here there are many rare ones you are hardly likely to see. You also get a glimpse of the tourist industry world-wide, and the beauty of the early postcard is well emphasized by the pictures. 96 large pages, with nearly 300 cards shown.

Once you have read at least some of these books, you will find in them other ways and means for enlarging your knowledge. You may wish to join a postcard club, and more of these are being formed each year. More and better catalogues are coming on the market, although you can often find the best buys amongst the cards they still OMIT at present. There are a number of regular periodicals, and the *Annual* published in Britain by the editor of *Picture Post Card Monthly* is full of interest, with every kind of feature you could think of. With all these aids, if you wish to, you can soon become master of the subject, and this will add much to your enjoyment, as well as directing your interest and your money in the most profitable way.

# Appendix 1. Abbreviations Used in Postcard Books, Catalogues, Lists and Auctions in Gt. Britain and U.S.A.

Where possible, these conform to International usage, as for example, given in *Everyman's Dictionary of Abbreviations*, edited by Dr. John Paxton.

A/D — Art Deco.
adv. — advertisement.
A/N — Art Nouveau.
aut. — autographed.
av. — average.
b/w — black and white.
c. — cards (number of).
cat. — catalogue value.
c.d.s. — circular date stamp.
chrome — modern colour printing.
chromo — chromo-lithograph, printed from stone.
col. — colour.
coll. — collotype printing.
c.o.r. — cash on receipt.
cnr/wr — corner wear.
cr. — crease.
c/up — close-up (or c.u.)
c.w.o. — cash with order.
ed/wr — edge wear.
emb. — embossed.
exh. — exhibition (in G.B.)
expo. — exposition (in U.S.A.)
ext. — exterior view.
G/a. — Gruss aus (Greetings from)
g.e. — gilt edge to card.
gl. — glossy finish.
h. — horizontal picture.
HTL — Hold to Light.
ill. — illustration.
I/N. — Individually numbered.
int. — interior view.
mk. — mark on card.
m/v. — multi-view card.
n.d. — no date.
n.s. — no stamp.
o.p. — original packet.
ovpt. — overprint.

o/w. — otherwise.
O.F. — Oilfacsim finish.
p/ — publisher (followed by name of).
PMC — Private Mailing Card (U.S.A.)
pmk. — postmark.
PPC — Picture Post Card.
p.s. — postal stationery.
ph. or pho. — photograph (also r.ph).
p.u. — postally used.
rev. — reverse side.
r.ph. — real photograph (gl. or matt).
s.a.e. — stamped addressed envelope.
s.a.f.e. — stamped addressed foolscap env.
sep. — sepia (a brown tone).
ser. — series.
sgd/ — signed (followed by artist's name).
sl. — slight.
st.sc. — street scene.
TM. — Trade Mark.
U. — Used.
u/b. — undivided back.
Un. — Unused.
v. — vertical picture.
vw. — view.
vign. — vignette (edge fades out).
w/a. — write away type of card
w.a.f. — with all faults.
w/f. — writing on front of card.
WW1. — World War One.
WW2. — World War Two.

*Condition of cards:*
M = Mint (see glossary).
VF = Very Fine.
F = Fine.
VG = Very Good.
G. = Good.
FR = Fair.
PR = Poor.
On no account should F be used for 'Fair'.

*Postcard Periods:* (in Gt. Britain)
1. = 1870-1899, The Early Postcard.
2. = 1900-1918, The Golden Age.
3. = 1919-1939, The Doldrums.
4. = 1940-1970, The Gradual Revival.
5. = 1971-today, The Modern Period.
See further in Chapter 4.

Some abbreviations can be confusing. In U.S.A. 'L.L' refers to large letter types, but in G.B. to the publisher Louis Levy.

# Appendix 2. Glossary of Definitions and Terms used in Postcard Collecting.

| | |
|---|---|
| airbrush | — colour applied by compressed air atomizer, giving a fine spray. |
| alumino | — a card so printed that the surface resembles aluminium in colour. |
| appliqué | — a card with another material or object fastened to its surface, see the chapter on Novelty Postcards. |
| back | — the side bearing stamp and address, the opposite side to the one carrying the picture, although small pictures sometimes appear on the address side too. |
| bas-relief | — a moulded picture giving a heightened embossed effect, the spaces behind being filled with a plaster when attached to the usually flat card backing. |
| bromide | — a paper and method used for processing early photographic cards, combining bromine with other elements, often resulting in a browner tone. |
| cartologist | — name often used in Britain to describe one who collects picture postcards. |
| cartophilist | — name used in France to describe one who collects picture postcards. In Britain, when postcards were hardly collected by anyone in the 1930s, this name was appropriated by collectors of cigarette cards, and so now exclusively applies to them. |
| chromo-litho | — a method of fine colour printing by the use of stones which produced results of a very high standard when executed efficiently. Shortened to 'chromo' colloquially in 1868. |
| close-up | — where the principal object on the card occupies more than about one-third of the available space. |
| collotype | — a printing method from photographs by means of a gelatin-surface plate which produced a smooth grainy result rather than the pattern of tiny dots visible where a half-tone screen is used. |
| composite sets | — by placing six to a dozen or more cards in a square or oblong the individual scenes on each card are seen to contribute to and be dwarfed by a larger picture, usually a portrait, to which each card contributes a portion of an arm, the head, etc. |
| court card | — a card especially used in Gt. Britain in the 1890s, but also in India and South Africa, which appears almost square in shape, its actual measurements officially being 115 x 89mm. See Ch. 4. |
| deltiologist | — name used in U.S.A., to describe one who collects picture postcards. |
| divided back | — where the back has a vertical line down the centre, with the address portion to the right, and the message portion to the left. First used in Britain in 1902, it was allowed in Germany in 1905, and U.S.A., in 1907. |
| early | — used too vaguely in the postcard world for any card with an undivided back. It should refer to cards *published* up to 1899 only. The date of postmark is not the deciding factor. |
| embossed | — a card where the design stands out in relief on the surface, adding to the realistic representation of the subject. |

Cards can be lightly embossed, but are best when they are deeply embossed.

**foreground** — the very front of the picture, so that a subject depicted there will be prominent and therefore exceptionally clear.

**frictograph** — a picture produced by rubbing the card with a silver coin, where before the surface was blank. It then resembles a pencil-drawn impression.

**front** — the picture side of the card, an opposite definition to that of the philatelist, for whom the front is the stamp/address side.

**full-out** — the subject alone occupies the surface of the card, usually with reference to heraldic devices such as crests and flags.

**glitter** — a glistening tinsel glued to the surface to heighten the outline, or attract the attention to a particular feature, such as decorations, flowers in the hair, etc.

**Gruss aus** — means 'Greetings from' in German. Especially applied to a type of multi-view card popular in Germany in the 1890s which had floral or similar decorations around the pictures, with the words 'Gruss aus . . .' in large ornamental letters.

**hand-coloured** — where a colour wash was applied to cards by a team of girls employed by a postcard publisher, who were paid a very small amount for each thousand cards they completed.

**hold-to-light** — when the card is held up to an electric light it seems to light up. There are basically two types: (1) windows, the moon, etc., are 'cut-out' on the top layer of card, and a thin layer of coloured paper is placed under these spaces to produce these 'light' areas; (2) a coloured layer of paper is placed between two especially translucent types of card, so that a sepia picture appears coloured when HTL. This latter type is called a 'transparency'. Hidden figures and objects also feature in this second type.

**inserts** — cards given away with magazines, and so 'inserted' within their pages upon publication. Usually these fall within the range of advertising, as promotion issues.

**installment** — these differ from composite sets. A set of three, four or more cards usually join each other end on, and when placed together make up a fish, animal or a comic scene. The idea was to send them in installments one by one so that the recipient had to guess what it was, or what would be the outcome of the comic situation.

**jewelled** — tiny coloured beads are appliquéd to costumes and dress to suggest jewellery; rubies, emeralds and diamonds, being the most usual and easy to simulate.

**kaleidoscope** — meaning a scope to produce beautiful forms. Produced in a similar way to a cut-out HTL, but the coloured paper is on a revolving disc between the layers of card. When rotated the colour pattern constantly changes, so that a dancer with a pretty dress seems to be in action, or a lighthouse seems to be sending out changing colour signals.

| | |
|---|---|
| large letters | — exactly what it says; the picture has a large letter caption, a name of a person or place, a word of greeting, etc. Some are very large, filled with pictures of actresses or views, some solid letters of the alphabet or a message. Sets of 26 large letters are often linked with names of famous people. |
| linens | — cards particularly produced in the U.S.A. in the 1930s to 1940s on a grained card which resembles linen in appearance. Along with 'chromes' they represent the gradual change to modern cards. |
| mechanical | — novelty cards with levers or tabs which make some parts move, bringing characters to life, as it were, or changing the scene on a card. |
| mezzotint | — a printing method whereby an engraving is made on copper or steel by scraping out areas pricked with tiny holes. Used on many early cards, it was a time-consuming process. |
| midget | — a very small postcard, measuring about $3\frac{1}{2}''$ x $2\frac{3}{4}''$. |
| mint | — a card in the pristine condition in which it left the printer, with no marks of an album or soiling of any kind, however slight. There are very few such mint cards, and when they are found it is usually because they have been protected by the original packet that contained them. Such cards may still not be 'perfect' because a mint card can have bad printing registration in its design or colouring. Unused cards are *not* mint ones. |
| montage | — the combining of several pictures on one card to tell a story, rather like a multi-view does for topographical cards. Also applied to pictures formed from parts of postage stamps cut up and appliquéd to a card as a 'stamp montage'. |
| officials | — issued by a recognized authority for purposes of promotion or advertising. Railways, shipping lines, hotels are the main groups where cards could be used for correspondence by patrons. |
| oilfacsim | — the surface of the card resembles an oil painting, reproducing the brushstroke finish so characteristic of this medium. |
| pioneer | — a term used mostly in U.S.A., to identify cards published before the Act of Congress of 19th May, 1898, effective 1st July, which allowed private postcards subject to certain conditions. |
| plate-sunk | — the central picture section of the card is 'sunk' (the reverse of embossing), in its relation to the frame of the card, which is usually left white and unprinted. |
| postal stationery | — cards issued by the government or its agencies with the postage stamp pre-printed on the back. Any item of stationery specially printed to show prepayment of postage. Although some of these were used by government departments, and so are 'officials', to apply this word to all postal stationery is incorrect, since much p.s. was printed to private order. |
| poster | — advertising cards which reproduce or resemble actual posters which were displayed on hoardings throughout the country. Usually identified by large display type of lettering for captions (see also semi-poster). |

| | |
|---|---|
| private mailing cards | — cards permitted with this wording on the back by Act of Congress in U.S.A. from 19th May 1898 (effective 1st July), until 24th December, 1901, when the regulation was relaxed and just 'Post Card' was allowed. Known as PMCs. |
| pull-outs | — cards with a pocket of various types from which can be pulled a strip of views of the place named or the subject depicted. |
| rare | — a word frequently misused, often in an attempt to obtain more money for a card than it is really worth. A card of which very few examples are *positively known* to survive. If only one or two examples are *positively known,* they would be 'extremely rare', if a dozen or so, 'very rare'. Because a dealer has not personally seen a card before certainly does not make it rare. |
| reward cards | — cards issued to be given as prizes or rewards, often by education authorities for work in schools well done. The backs are often printed with details rather than a postcard back. |
| scarce | — a card not available in great numbers. Difficult for collectors to find, but not in any degree 'rare'. There could still be several thousands extant, but it may be much sought after, and once collectors get a copy they don't easily let it go again, thus creating a 'scarcity' on the market. Quite a different type of rating from the word 'rare' which is not subject to market forces, but relates purely to actual survival of copies. |
| section cards | — see installment cards. |
| semi-poster | — lacking the prominent caption lettering which marks the poster proper, but still showing some of its characteristics. Some lettering is *incorporated in* the design, though smaller and subdued, so that it does not depend on titles and captions outside the design (below it or to one side) to advertise it. A picture merely incorporating the product in the design would not in itself be sufficient to classify it as a 'semi-poster'. |
| sepia | — a picture in a brown tone, even approaching black at times, and used generally to describe collotypes, gravure processes, etc. |
| sleepers | — good and interesting types of cards which do not attract many collectors at present, but may have a potential future. |
| undivided back | — having no vertical line to delineate spaces for message and address. The back was to be used solely for the name, address and stamp. |
| unique | — the only one in existence, and safely said only of a hand-drawn original postcard. Can never be 'nearly unique'. |
| vignette | — from a little picture or embellishment has come to mean for postcards a small picture not enclosed by a border, and shading off into the unprinted section, often available for writing the message. |
| write-away | — an early form intended to aid the writer by its picture, and often starting a sentence for him which is a pun on the picture itself. 'I am leaving this . . .'— rider is thrown from horse in picture. |

## Appendix 3. How Many Postcards Survive Until Today?

This is an extremely difficult question to answer, and any calculation must inevitably involve some guesswork at one point or another, so what is said here is solely with the aim of producing some *reasonable* estimate.

We may ask, why bother at all to consider such a question? That some viewpoint is desirable is shown by two factors: (1) Many writers have continually stated that the supply of picture postcards will soon run out, and that as collectors take them into their collections, and do not release them again at anything like the inflow rate, a serious shortage will soon appear. Perhaps this has been seized upon by some dealers to goad their customers into buying more cards, or even to pay a higher price for special ones—"it is rare", or "I haven't had this card through my hands in the last three years". (2) In their excellent book, *Picture Postcards of the Golden Age*, Tonie and Valmai Holt suggested (p.43) that perhaps about 35 million cards survive, based upon a 1% survival rate from 1900-1910. They admitted this was merely a stab at a figure, but it has since been quoted without its context as a quite definitive estimate of the number of cards, in magazines with large circulations, and this is a pity. The idea that there are so few cards available therefore needs to be corrected, and that is the aim of this brief investigation.

We can base our calculations upon fairly precise returns for Gt. Britain issued by the Post Office from the year the picture postcard first began to appear until 1916, when a break in records was caused by the First World War. That is a suitable period, however, for it covers most of the Golden Age, but we will need to remember that the millions of cards issued in the 1920s and 1930s are not included in these statistics. Some percentages of private postcards as distinct from business use have had to be estimated for years where the Post Office did not have a figure:

| Post Office Year | Millions of P.Cs. | % Private | Private P.Cs. Most Picture |
|---|---|---|---|
| Year ended 31st March 1895 | 312.8 | E 30% | 93.8* |
| ,, ,, 1896 | 314.5 | E 37% | 116.4* |
| ,, ,, 1897 | 336.5 | 44% | 148.1* |
| ,, ,, 1898 | 360.4 | E 50% | 180.2* |
| ,, ,, 1899 | 382.2 | E 54% | 206.4* |
| ,, ,, 1900 | 400.3 | 58% | 232.2 |
| ,, ,, 1901 | 419.0 | E 60% | 251.4 |
| ,, ,, 1902 | 444.9 | 65% | 289.2 |
| ,, ,, 1903 | 488.9 | 69% | 337.3 |
| ,, ,, 1904 | 613.7 | 77% | 472.5 |
| ,, ,, 1905 | 734.5 | 81% | 594.5 |
| ,, ,, 1906 | 800.3 | 84% | 672.2 |
| ,, ,, 1907 | 831.4 | E 85% | 706.7 |
| ,, ,, 1908 | 858.3 | E 86% | 738.2 |
| ,, ,, 1909 | 860.0 | E 87% | 748.2 |
| ,, ,, 1910 | 866.8 | E 88% | 762.8 |
| ,, ,, 1911 | 871.4 | E 89% | 775.6 |
| ,, ,, 1912 | 905.5 | E 90% | 815.0 |
| ,, ,, 1913 | 899.0 | E 90% | 809.0 |
| ,, ,, 1914 | 926.5 | E 90% | 833.9 |
| ,, ,, 1915 | 880.0 | E 90% | 792.0 |
| | 13,506.9 | | 10,576.0 |

Deduct for use of plain postcards, esp. years*      576.0

                                                                   10,000.0

Add unused cards, ratio of at least 1 to 1      10,000.0

Total picture pc's issued in G.B. 1894-1915, say      20,000.0 million

or an *average* of approximately almost one thousand million each year.

It is interesting to notice the comment about the picture postcard in the report for the year ended 31st March 1907. "The growth in popularity of the picture postcard apparently reached its climax two years ago, and the rate of increase appears to have returned to the normal". But it will be noticed from the figures that it remained near to that high level right to the end of our period, and most probably was maintained, if not increased a little, during the years of World War One.

I have collected a number of similar statistics for Germany, France and other European countries, the United States of America and Japan, but none of them are complete enough to show tables. We can get reasonable estimates from these, however, which include a total of 2,360 million world-wide for 1901, 7,000 million world-wide by 1905, with one postman delivering 100 cards to one person in just a single postal delivery. Some countries were earlier off the mark, with Germany reaching 1,161 million in the year 1903/4, whilst in that same year U.S.A. reached 770 million and Japan 487 million. Even as early as 1900/01 the German post office dealt with 736 million cards, when in Britain the figure was not much more than half that figure delivered. By 1910 it was reported that two and a half million postcards were sold every day in the U.S.A.

The estimate given by Tonie and Valmai Holt of "between 1 and 3 million postcards passed through the post daily" would therefore seem to refer only to Gt. Britain, since this figure is approximately 1½ million per day based on the Post Office figures, mostly picture ones. But this does not include those *not* posted, nor this vast number throughout the world. We can safely say that all other countries put together received more than six times as many cards as the 10,000 million in Gt. Britain during those 20 years (actually 21, but we will keep things simple). In fact, the partial figures suggest an estimate nearer to seven or eight times. But taking six times, or 60,000 million, adding on the same figure for unused cards, and then the 20,000 million for Britain, we come to a grand total of 140,000 million picture postcards in 20 years world-wide.

If we said that just 1% of these survived, we would arrive at a figure of 1,400 million (one thousand, four hundred million) rather than a mere 35 million, but judging from the number of collections that still come on the market just as they were built up seventy years ago, and have done for many years past, it would seem a much larger percentage has survived. True, for more than 20 years little market could be found for postcards, and they must have been destroyed in their millions, and even now many persons throw them out because they do not know their value or cannot be bothered with them, when, perhaps, they have an entire house contents to dispose of. But I do not think it is unreasonable to suppose that 5% have survived, and this would produce a figure of seven thousand million cards (7,000 million), or in the reckoning in the U.S.A. 7 billion.

Obviously, it is this percentage survival rate that makes such a critical difference, but even if it is the lowest figure of 1%, 1,400 million cards is a very considerable number, so that even if several persons, as reported, do have one million cards each, there are still plenty remaining to go round, without fear that a sudden shortage will hit the market.

Of course, when we consider the vast *variety* of cards which were published, quantities of certain types will not be great. Further, if we examine the G.B. figures again, it will quickly be obvious that for every six cards surviving from 1905, there will only be two from 1899, given similar ratios throughout. Remember too, that we have not included any cards published after World War One.

# Appendix 4. Important Postcard Dates

1861    Lipman's private postal card issued in U.S.A. (see ch. 4).

1865    Dr. Heinrich von Stephan's idea for a postcard is put forward, but rejected.

1869    Austria's first plain postcard issued, promoted by Dr. Emanuel Herrmann (1st October).

1870    North Germany's first plain postcard (1st June); followed shortly by small picture cards in Germany.
Switzerland and France first issue postcards.
Britain's first plain postcard (1st October); Northern Polytechnic Advertising postcard (1st October); Day's series of coloured Christmas postcards.

1871    Belgium, Holland, Heligoland and Canada first issue postcards.

1872    Russia first issues postcards; possible first view cards designed by Frank Borich issued in Switzerland; Doré's advertising picture postcard issued by Grant & Co., of Fleet St., London, with one known copy clearly postmarked March 18th 1872.

1873    Spain and Japan first issue postcards; Germany issues lengthy series of views on p.s. cards; U.S.A. issues first government postals (May), and advertisement postcard appears for U.S. Interstate Industrial Exposition in Chicago.

1882    France issues map postcard for Pneumatic Post (see illustration).

1889    First Eiffel Tower postcard.

1894    Private picture postcards allowed in Britain (1st September); Experimental Snowdon card issued by Tuck.

1897    Queen Victoria Diamond Jubilee postcards issued (very scarce but not rare).

1898    Private Mailing Cards permitted in U.S.A. (1st July).

1899    Normal size private picture postcards permitted in Britain (1st November); Firm of Raphael Tuck first enters picture postcard market.

1901    PMC no longer needed on U.S. cards (24th December).

1902    Divided back first introduced in Britain by F. Hartmann, other publishers follow slowly over a period of many months.

1905    Germany introduces divided back.

1907    U.S.A. introduces divided back (1st March).

1918    Inland rate for picture postcards increased from $\frac{1}{2}$d to 1d in Britain (3rd June).

1921    Inland rate again increased from 1d to $1\frac{1}{2}$d (13th June).

1922    Reduced again to 1d after much protest (24th May).

1926    New maximum and minimum sizes adopted in Britain, min 4″ x 2¾″, max. 5⅞″ x 4⅛″ (international size).


# Appendix 5. 'Postcard' in the Principal Languages

This list may help you to identify the country from which a postcard comes, if you do not know where the place is, and no printing details are given.

| | |
|---|---|
| Bilhete Postal | — Portugal and colonies. |
| Brevkort (some Brefkort) | — Scandinavia: Denmark, Norway, Sweden. |
| Briefkaart | — Netherlands, Dutch colonies, parts S. Africa. |
| Brjefspjald | — Iceland. |
| Carta Posta | — Ireland (Erse). |
| Carta Postala/Carte Postala | — Roumania. |
| Carte Postale | — France and colonies. |

| | | |
|---|---|---|
| Cartolina Postale | — | Italy and colonies. |
| Dopisnice | — | Czechoslovakia (also used Carte Postale). |
| Kartka Pocztowa | — | Poland. |
| Levelezö-Lap | — | Hungary. |
| Llythyr-Gerdyn | — | Wales. |
| Nowehcka Kapta | — | Bulgaria. |
| Noytobar Kaptoyka | — | Russia. |
| Postikortti | — | Finland. |
| Postkaart | — | Belgium (usually with Carte Postale as well). |
| Postkarte | — | Germany and colonies/states, Austria. |
| Poŝtkartoj | — | Esperanto. |
| Tarjeta Postal | — | Spain and colonies, most of South and Central America. |

For a number of countries where more than one principal language is spoken, the word will appear in those languages. Brazil has fluctuated between the Spanish and Portugese titles, for example, sometimes using both. Swiss cards are identified by the use of three languages—French, German and Italian.

## Appendix 6.  Identifying Some Outstanding Postcard Publishers

**A.N.C.** American News Co. N.Y.
**B.B.** Birn Bros, London.
**B.B. & Oi. L.** Bruno Berger & Ottilie, Leipzig.
**B & Co.** Bamforth & Co.
**B. & D.** Blum & Degen, London.
**B.K.W.** Brüder-Kohn, Vienna.
**C.T.K.** Carl Kunzli, Tobler, Zurich.
**CWF & Co.** C. W. Faulkner & Co. London.
**E.A.S.** E. A. Schwerdtfeger, Berlin & London.
**E.G.Co.** Edward Gross Co., N.Y.
**E.L.D.** E. Le Deley, Paris.
**E.T.W.D.** E. T. W. Dennis & Son, Yorkshire.
**F.H.** Franz Huld Co. N.Y.
**G.A.Co.** Gibson Art Co. Cincinnati.
**GD & D.** Gottschalk, Dreyfus & Davis, Munich, London, N.Y.
**G & P.** Gale & Polden, Aldershot.
**H & B.** Harding & Billing, Australia & N.Z.
**I.A. Co.** Inter-Art Co. London.
**J.B.Co.** J. Beagles & Co. London.
**J.J.** Julian Freres (Bros), Geneva.
**J.V.** J. Valentine, Dundee, Canada etc.
**K.F.** Kunzli Freres (Bros), Paris.
**KN.** (joined) Knackstedt & Nather, Hamburg.

**L.L.** Louis Levy, Paris & London.
**M & B.** Meissner & Buch, Leipzig and London.
**M & Co.** Misch & Co. London.
**M & L.** Millar & Lang, Glasgow.
**M.M.** M. Munk, Vienna.
**N.D.** Neurdein & Co. Paris.
**N & O. D.** Nenke & Ostermaier, Dresden (Photochromie often above).
**O.Z.** Ottmar Zieher, Munich.
**P. Co.** Photochrom Co. Kent.
**P.F.B.** Paul Finkenrath, Berlin.
**P.Z.** Photoglob Co. Zurich.
**R & N.** Reinthal & Newman, N.Y.
**R.P.C.** Rotary Photo Co. London.
**R.T. & S.** Raphael Tuck & Son, London, N.Y. etc.
**S.H.** S. Hildesheimer & Co. London.
**S.L. & Co.** S. Langsdorf & Co. N.Y.
**T.E.L. or Th.E.L.** Theodore Eismann, Leipzig.
**T.S.N.** Theodore Stroefer, Nuremberg.
**U.** Ullmann, Man. Co. N.Y.
**V & S.** Valentine & Sons, Dundee, Scotland.
**WH.** W. Hagelberg, Berlin & London.
**W & K.** Wildt & Kray, London.

# SUBJECT INDEX

hand-coloured 5, 85.
handling cards, with care 79.
hand-painted 17, 29, 31, 39.
Hands across Sea 48.
Hansom cabs 58, 70, 71.
harbours 11, 63.
hats 29, 30, 36.
heraldic 23, 40, 51.
Herrmann, Dr. E. 16.
history, local 11.
hobbies 5, 6.
hold-to-light 36, 37, 85.
hospitals 11, 63.
hotel/inns 7, 9, 21, 57, 70, 71.
houses 9, 65, 70, 72.
hunts 11, 46, 67.

illuminated art 27, 49.
India 61, 69.
Indians, Red 25, 36, 81.
industry 11.
inserts 22, 85.
installment sets 38, 85.
intermediate size 19.
investment 6, 73, 75, 80.
Ireland 19, 50, 60.
islands 67, 68.
Italy 19, 55, 69, 73.

Jacob's ladders 71.
Japan 25, 28, 40, 55, 64, 89.
jewels 36, 39, 85.
Jubilee, Q. V. 75.

Kaiser 38, 44.

language of . . . 45, 46.
large letter 37, 86.
last . . . 70.
Levy, Louis 46, 59, 83.
lifeboats 63.
lighthouses 63, 68.
Lipman postal card 15.
literary 44, 46.
Loch Ness monster 68.
London 8, 18, 19, 35, 45, 57, 61, 65, 66,
   69, 70, 71, 73, 75.
London life 12, 13.

Man, Isle of 66, 69.
maps 10, 25, 34, 38, 53, 56, 58, 63, 64,
   72.
markets 11.
match boxes 69.
materials used 36.
mechanicals 36, 37, 86.
medals 53, 54.
menu postcards 62, 63.
messages 42, 57, 63, 66, 68, 72.

midget cards 39, 86.
military 53-55.
mills 11, 25.
mint, definition 86.
mirror 36, 38, 67.
models 36, 39, 61, 69, 70.
motor cars 11, 34, 58, 71, 72.
motor cycles 69.
mountains 34, 63, 64, 69.
Mucha, A. 26, 77.
multi-views 18, 42, 44.
music 5, 42, 43, 44.
music hall 41, 43.

navy 54, 55, 56, 64.
Nelson, Lord 56.
Netherlands 28, 63.
newspapers 11, 24, 54.
New York 59, 72, 73.
notepaper, pictorial 15.
novelty cards 36-39.
numbered cards 69.
numbers surviving 73, 88, 89.

officials 21, 60, 61, 62, 86.
Oilette 82.
Oilfacsims 86.
oldest . . . 70.
Olympic Games 45.
orders/medals 52-54.
origins of postcard 15, 80.

pageants 11.
Palestine 36, 54, 70.
Panama Canal 72.
Paris 17, 25, 30, 64, 69, 70, 73.
patriotic 48.
Peel, John 66, 67.
performing groups 43.
photography 8, 9, 11, 12, 40, 41, 46,
   58, 66, 68, 71.
photo-origin 9.
picnics 12, 43.
Picture P.C. Monthly 71, 82.
pierrots 43.
piers 61.
ping-pong 33, 46.
pioneers 19, 81, 86.
playing cards 45, 46, 53.
PMC's 19, 20, 87.
pneumatic post 64.
polar exploration 63.
police 11.
political 44, 49-51, 81.
postal stationery 16, 19, 86.
postcard albums 69, 79.
postcard collecting 18, 46, 48, 69, 78.
postcard fairs 73.
postcard, first 15, 16, 17.

93

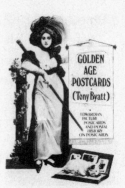